VOICES FROM THE NIGHT

The Power and Promise of Community Change

by

James E. Copple

Dedication

We are a blended family. Between Colleen and me, we have eight children and eighteen grandchildren. Those twenty-six individuals each have their own voice and they often call in the night. I am more proud than I can dare express of what each of them mean to me. I have watched our eight children and their spouses mature and grow into adults that make a difference in their families, their work, and their communities. I have the same hope and promise for our grandchildren.

To all of them, I dedicate this book
Jamie and Tom, Jessica and Jason, Karin and Scott, B.J. and Maggie, Julie and Paulo, Maureen, Michael, and Steven and to the eighteen grandchildren: Xidis, Brendan, Jameson, Annicka, Park, Indie, Milo, Aaron, Jordan, Isabel, Elyxzia, Maizzie Mae, Anyx, Kayzia, Jackson, Jones, Peyton, and Caroline.

Contents

Foreword

Voices from the Night. Such a suggestive title. You will certainly find it challenging. In the beginning, this book was about Jim's experiences doing street interventions in Wichita, Kansas riding with the Gang Unit four nights a week, while holding down his day job as Special Assistant to the Superintendent of Schools. After having a 15-year-old die in his hands following a drive-by shooting his first night on the streets with the Gang Unit, Jim never turned back. As he knelt down and cradled the boy's head in his hands, the blood soaking his khaki pants, the boy whispered his last words: "Help me."

Such moments are defining, life changing; they take over. Project Freedom, the community gang and substance abuse coalition Jim ran at the time, set the standard for innovation, in part because of his hands-on approach, he personally interviewed hundreds of kids on the streets. The gangs gave him a street name, 'Clipboard' because he was always taking notes or handing out jobs from, yes, his clipboard. That was in the early nineties. Jim has added two more decades of experience to his resumé and his message, grounded now in national and international policy work on crime, violence, gangs, substance abuse and poverty eradication. As his brother likes to say, he will never be out of a job.

However, this last decade has been unusual, even by Jim's standards. As his partner in business, development and in life for the last decade, I have had an inside track, having experienced Africa at his side. Jim is a big thinker, a doer. He throws himself into a situation in order to truly understand it, to listen, to absorb the truth of a situation, a person's lot, a community's cry for help, a nation on the verge of taking flight or of crashing. In the academic world, he refers to it as taking an ethnographic approach. You have to be there, you have to ask questions to understand and listen to actually learn. In the context of his faith, it is an incarnational approach, truly living in the world, fully observant and fully engaged. It doesn't happen in the easy places, it happens in the hardest, most abandoned places.

Jim experiences life in the dust and heat of the drought in Kenya or the gun shots fired at his vehicle on the Ethiopia Somali border. Jim agonizes with the women who tell us when asked, that even though the feeding program intended to help them survive the famine should be sufficient, they don't have enough food to get them to the end of the month, because when their starving neighbors come to ask for food, they do not turn them away. "What would Jesus have us do?" Life changing, humbling, compelling experiences thrust us forward to do what we can, to be smart, sensitive, wise, unshakeable, stubborn and unyielding in responding in whatever way we can, in every way that we can.

Whether it is children, women, the disabled, the stigmatized, the rejected, the other, in our backyards and across the globe, we are responsible to do what we can to make the world a better place. We can do that by throwing one starfish at a time back into the ocean and we can be smart about changing the bigger picture systems and policies that multiply the effect millions of times over. Both are important. They don't happen in isolation from each other. They inform each other. This book will take you from the personal to the practical to the policy framework and back again for they are circular.

The dialogue and application of empathy has progressed from compassion to aid to development to sustainability and now to resilience. Being effective is important. Good intentions are the beginning point, responding appropriately, with the tools to "do no harm" and to actually "do good" are critical.

Voices from the Night will break your heart, but it will also inspire you about the resilience of the human heart, the human condition. In the midst of despair, there is grace, faith, leadership, generosity, humility and hope. It will challenge you, motivate you to think bigger, think smarter, use your best gifts to respond to the world we live in, to step up, to fully engage, to be that faithful presence, to walk with your brothers and sisters, to bear their burdens with them, to stand with them in solidarity, as voyagers, as seekers in this world.

Seeker, that word means so much to both of us. It's the name of our sailboat, our refuge, our place of healing. That word tells you a lot about us and about this book. Seekers are looking for truth, enlightenment, meaning, purpose, understanding, and direction. We are seeking to act on what we see, what we know and what we learn. We are seeking to be faithful doers of the word, not hearers only. To be His hands and His feet, with humility, but with the highest expectations that we do the best we can with the tools that we have. When those tools are not good enough, we figure out what the next iteration should be. We are not complacent; we are not arrogant; we are listeners who take the time to be still, to hear, observe, engage and reflect. We are companions who lift one another's burdens, who mourn with those who mourn, who collect trash in the slums of Nairobi side-by-side with our youth leaders, and who plant seeds in the garden project with our HIV/AIDS support groups in Swaziland. We are sojourners who take the time to talk to that scary looking teenager down the street, to ask their name and engage them; who intervene with an abusive parent or spouse in a public or a private place; who proudly stand with our gay son, a person of deep faith.

Nothing about this is particularly easy, but it is, to quote Rev. Dr. Wilson Goode, "the difference between living a life of success and a life of significance." Not because we need or crave approval or recognition, or are trying to assuage guilt, but because it is who we are, as disciples seeking to live out the word, listening to the winds of the spirit, and responding boldly.

Colleen K. Copple
Partner (In All of Life)

Come Along Side - A Definition

Just what does that phrase mean? You will see it often in this book and it is a critical part of my vocabulary and belief system. It describes a strategic approach as well as a bridge to empathic understanding of another person's predicament - a difficult and trying situation. The phrase responds to approaches that seek to do something for another, approaches that create some kind of dependency and, alas, approaches that exert complete control. To come along side expresses a volitional action, it validates a position of equality and it accents a process or a journey.

My career path is about coming alongside the dispossessed, the impoverished, the broken, and the wounded. To be in journey along side of the oppressed is to recognize that you bring skills, gifts, and capacity that can strengthen or contribute to the welfare of those you engage. Further, to come along side suggests that you have as much to learn from the other as the other has to learn from you. It is a bridge bound by love, grace, and empathy

Preface

*The wind blows wherever it pleases. You hear its sound,
but you cannot tell where it comes from or where it is
going.
So it is with everyone born of the Spirit. (John 3:8)*

Perhaps the most significant element of America's current economic condition and our participation in the global economic meltdown is that children are at the epicenter of the suffering here and abroad. Children are not simply bystanders or random casualties who occasionally fall victim to poor economic planning, inability to access education, and healthcare or parental abandonment because of disease or war. Poverty, drugs, and disease have left a body count that has robbed our future. Children require support and an environment where they can grow and mature into contributing adults. We continue to fail in this effort.

Yet, from the battlefield, there emerge voices that continue to surprise us for their clarity, resilience, and persistence. They are the voices of our children. Our children struggle to escape the pain caused by isolation and the reality that they have been relegated to the waste heap of lost priorities. As adults, policy makers, funders, and bureaucrats traverse the fields of other priorities, our children cry out for attention and demand that we listen. This book seeks to resurrect our children's voices and allow their souls to speak, thereby inspiring action. To achieve this we must find within ourselves the power to consistently communicate who and what our priorities must be and to act with passion and urgency.

On a late Saturday evening, the Gang Unit of the Wichita Police Department received a call requesting that I be taken to the site of a domestic violence dispute involving a known gang member. It was an unusual request; our organization was seldom brought into domestic violence disputes, even if they involved gang members. That evening, I was riding in a squad car with the gang unit officers, Kent Bauman and Brad Carey. We arrived in a neighborhood with broken streetlights and the acrid smell of waste from a vacant lot that made the darkness seem more vivid. Three squad cars were parked in front of the house and a number of officers stood in the doorway awaiting our arrival.

As I entered the house, I saw a handcuffed gang member leaning against a kitchen counter who was shouting one expletive after another. As I approached, he leaned back and spit in my direction. His aim was as poor as his false bravado. His three-day drug binge using cocaine and alcohol left him wasted. An officer told me that the girlfriend wanted to speak with me. As she sat on the couch surrounded by three children, a medic was treating her badly bruised and cut face. Her right eye was swollen where her boyfriend had pounded it repeatedly. I knelt down beside her and asked if there was anything more we could do for her at that moment. She asked if he were going to be arrested. I said, "Yes, and we will do what we can to keep him there for a while." I asked why she called *me* and how did she know to call *me.* She held in her hand the Project Freedom phone number she had taken from a tag line of a Partnership for a Drug-Free America public service advertisement. She had written it down several weeks before in the event she ever needed it. I was startled by the resourcefulness of this young woman and the effectiveness of the TV spot. It had captured her attention.

As we discussed a strategy to provide her shelter that would guarantee her safety, I felt this tug on my shirtsleeve. I turned to look into the eyes of a beautiful four-year-old girl with curly hair and a yellow ribbon pulling a section into a neat ponytail. In a determined voice, asked a question that I will never forget. "Mister, can you get me out of here?" The question surprised me. It was not simply about satisfying the immediate need for a bed and some sleep. It was a call for rescue - it was a call that suggested confidence in my capacity to get her relief and help. To her, I was like a fireman pulling her from a fire that was engulfing her and destroying her tomorrows.

A colleague took her hand, and we walked her out of the room and onto the front porch. Within a few minutes, I heard laughter and giggling as my colleague distracted her from the ugly business the adults were conducting in the house. Mom and children were rescued - for the moment. They were placed in a shelter that could help them for a maximum of seven days. The boyfriend was out on bail within 24 hours of his arrest. Two days after his release, a judge issued a restraining order that he violated with impunity on at least three separate occasions. Our coalition, Project Freedom, sprang into action, working to provide a permanent job and residence for the mom. We placed each of the children in a different school with transportation provided by the district.

Within the next month, the police arrested the boyfriend for the murder of a rival gang member and he is currently spending a hard 40 years in a Kansas penitentiary. Mom and children, with support from the community coalition, are doing fine. Mom has a job, and the children have found new hope in friends, schools and a community prepared to give them a chance to succeed.

The image of a four-year-old asking to be rescued from a crack house has become a metaphor for our efforts to advocate for children. The conditions that evening were horrific: anger, blood, handcuffs on the boyfriend (a gang member), and people filling out their bureaucratic forms. As I turned to call a social worker, the four-year-old stretched out her arms and asked to be held. She was badly soiled, and I found myself hesitating. Then her brown eyes connected with my brown eyes, and suddenly we all had red eyes. She would be rescued. Help was on the way. I am often tormented by the moms who cannot help their children; by the dads who struggle to put food on the table; by the siblings who worry about their brothers and sisters as they walk to school and by the neighborhoods who define their future as futile. They hang on by a thread and hope that the next crisis will not break that thread. This fear is far more acute than any culture or civilization should tolerate.

"Mister, can you get me out of here?" The question, in this case, had a positive outcome. In many other cases, however, the answer is not always as positive. The number of children dying across the globe in homes and streets is of an epidemic nature. Twenty percent of American children live in poverty and are on the brink of homelessness. Global statistics point to the harsh reality that each day the sun rises in the East and sets in the West three thousand children die from hunger or disease. We are not responding with the passion and anger that normally accompanies the death, mutilation or abuse of a child because the sheer numbers have produced a numbing affect. The figures simply defy explanation, much less reaction. For whatever reason, the media, our acceptance of a culture of violence, or the normalization of violent behavior, the needed outrage when a child or family is victimized by violence or drugs is lacking. Even workers in this arena find ways to retreat into our shells of callousness and detachment in order to better serve our clients. The prospect of being wounded by too intimate a contact with human suffering is unsettling and uncomfortable.

Regardless of where we live and work, there are children and adults in our communities, citizens living within our communities who are looking to volunteers, neighbors, clergy, and professionals to find a way to get them out. In all of our lives, there are children asking, "Mister, can you get me out of here?"

These voices from the night are often powerless and lack the capacity to alter their situation and advocate for their own position. They are usually travelers through the various systems and relationships created by social services, educational services, and criminal justice agencies. They stop at society's stations of care, juvenile courts and health care providers. They receive minimum care. Often the media, policymakers, and the callous stereotype them as children of the lazy and shiftless.

We meet, contact, and touch these victims in isolation and in disparate responses. Agencies and non-profits are notorious for their lack of coordinated thinking when delivering programs and services. They have lost their commitment to build relationships. An agency's or government's ability to construct a collaborative system is often met by legal barriers and efforts to protect the privacy of juveniles. Well-intended social and legal policies run amok, leaving behind ruined and destroyed lives. The very institutions created to help and rescue children often become the forces that enslave them.

Throughout these pages, we will explore the condition of our world's children and youth. We will discover ways that individuals and communities have sought to rescue them and be encouraged to take specific and concrete action to hear and respond to the voices from the night. As a global community and as a people we are too good and too resourceful to allow any child to be lost to the night. These voices from the night will find their strength as the adults in our communities make a commitment to the *least of these,* bringing joy and hope to be enjoyed in the light of day. Surely, the winds of change for our children will blow. We will hear its sound, but its source and its direction can only surprise us.

Chapter One – Mission Rescue

Rescue:

1 a: To free from confinement, danger, or evil: SAVE, DELIVER; b: to take (as a prisoner) forcibly from legal custody

2 a: to recover (as a prize) by force; b: to deliver (as a place besieged) by force of arms – rescue – rescuer n syn DELIVER, REDEEM, RANSOM, RECLAIM, SAVE:

RESCUE implies freeing from imminent danger by prompt or vigorous action;

DELIVER implies release usually of a person from confinement, temptation, slavery, suffering;

REDEEM implies releasing from bondage or penalties by giving what is demanded or necessary;

RANSOM specifically applies to buying out of captivity;

RECLAIM suggests a bringing back to a former state or condition someone or something abandoned or debased;

SAVE may replace any of the forgoing terms; it may further imply a preserving or maintaining for usefulness or continued existence.[1]

Charlene, a twelve-year old middle-school student from Wichita, Kansas came to school with a bruise over her eye. Her teacher noticed and asked about it. Charlene, responded that she had fallen and hit her head on the bed. The teacher was not convinced. She pursued the topic, and Charlene provided a dubious excuse, simply saying she had tripped over a throw rug. The teacher, knowing something of Charlene's home situation, suspected abuse, and the law obligated her to report Charlene's condition. She met with the principal, who was legally obligated to report the incident to the State Office of Social and Rehabilitation Services (SRS). Within six hours, SRS had completed an intervention and moved Charlene to a foster home until a thorough investigation could be conducted.

While the case was under investigation, Charlene was arrested for shoplifting. The arresting officer found her in possession of a small amount of marijuana and significant amounts of acid. Charlene was taken to the community children's home to await a hearing in juvenile court. During the stay at the children's home, Charlene met with three separate social workers: a

---

[1] *Webster's* p 730.

school social worker, a social worker assigned by SRS and a social worker assigned by the juvenile court. At no time, did those three social workers ever meet to discuss Charlene's case.

When Charlene appeared before the judge, a court appointed attorney and guardian *ad litem* was assigned to her case. The judge ordered a substance abuse evaluation conducted by a social worker operating out of a publicly funded treatment facility in the community. The judged ordered Charlene into drug treatment and placed her on six months probation. She had a previous offense for vandalism, unknown to any of the social workers, teacher, or principal. The only one in the process who knew about the previous offense was the juvenile court social worker. During her three weeks on this journey, Charlene was not in her middle school. Her teachers, the principal, and the staff were completely out of the communication loop regarding her status. They didn't know if she was going to return, be transferred, or dis-enrolled.

After finishing drug treatment, Charlene lived in a foster home, returned to school and tried to pick up the various pieces of her young life. Although Charlene never sold drugs nor had the intention, other students knew she'd been busted for drug dealing. She was a "hot" commodity among her peers. Because of the rumors, Charlene became a target for two separate girl gangs operating in her school. Charlene sought out another teacher for advice and counsel on how to avoid the peer pressure that would move her into gang life. The teacher, ignorant of Charlene's past, simply dismissed her remarks as attention-getting and told her to be strong and she could resist.

Two weeks after visiting the teacher, Charlene was "jumped" into a gang. Three weeks later, she was arrested for vandalism and destruction of property. A judge ordered Charlene to be placed in a juvenile detention center, where, after receiving a physical, the doctor determined that Charlene was pregnant. So, this 13 year-old girl had a criminal record and soon would also have a child. She was provided counseling, medical assistance, and placed in the school district's teen pregnancy resource center. Within six months of giving birth to her child, Charlene enrolled in a school district alternative school. She gave up gang life and focused on the welfare of her child. Foster parents cared for her and her child. But at sixteen, Charlene dropped out of the alternative school. Three months later, Charlene was again arrested, this time for armed robbery, and found in possession of six ounces of crack cocaine. Charlene was again placed in juvenile detention, her two-year-old child was placed in another foster home, and the cycle began all over.

This story, filled with a depressing series of catastrophic events, is the story of many serious and habitual offenders that occupy America's prisons and juvenile detention centers. When interviewing them, the failure of numerous systems to adequately and comprehensively address their needs always strikes me anew. In no way is this a dismissal of individual responsibility. Yet, we must admit that when at-risk children enter our community and state driven systems - welfare, schools, courts, or foster care - there is simply no mechanism to alert the community that it is dealing with a potential habitual offender. Many of these offenders like Charlene enter our community systems without regard to choice or option. They are placed or assigned, and while they may meet compassionate and sensitive caseworkers, they become numbers in an already overburdened system.

Charlene's story and the thousands like her found in nearly all of our communities raise the issue and question of how we create a sense of urgency and a mechanism for communication among agencies involved in the lives of children. No one can be involved in Charlene's experience or in the experience of the four-year-old in a crack house and not feel passion, urgency to act, and the need to communicate the needs and conditions of their predicament. Much of what is to be found in our understanding of rescue emphasizes the need to create a climate of urgency. The most critical challenge to a community dealing with its "at-risk" youth population is the inability for various systems to communicate with each other. Privacy regulations "protecting" juveniles, created difficulties for educators, and social workers to acquire information from courts or other community systems. Communities have experimented with different approaches to information sharing but are usually thwarted by the balance between privacy and community responsibility.

Imagine what might have been done had the systems dealing with Charlene had a coordinated strategy that would have dealt with Charlene as *whole* child instead of Charlene as the *abused* child, Charlene the *juvenile delinquent*, Charlene the *drug user*, Charlene the *drug dealer*, Charlene the *teenage mom*. Had the various influences or system interveners in Charlene's life been talking with each other, then maybe Charlene would have had a chance.

Charlene's story and the story of the young family experiencing gang-related domestic violence are simply variations on a basic story. It illustrates both the lack of communication between victims and service providers and the need to build individual, community, and national mechanisms for promoting communication that will create change and build environments where children can be rescued. The most consistent complaint from service recipients is the failure of systems to adequately communicate with each other or with the intended recipient. This failure complicates their capacity to provide relief, and further and perhaps most significantly at this time in our history, is that it leads to duplication of effort and a profound waste of resources.

Mobilizing the Rescuers

Regardless of the problems facing our children in our neighborhoods, they need consistent and persistent voices from diverse sectors of the community. These voices need consistently to express the urgency of action, the passion of the mission, and the hope we offer communities. Volunteers, clergy, business leaders, teachers, directors of afterschool programs and coaches of youth sports, all need to be building on the strengths of our children and admonishing them in all phases of their life to resist behavior that is destructive and counter-productive.

Our children are not stupid. They understand the futility of a single strategy aimed at informing them about the dangers of drug abuse, teen pregnancy, youth violence or school failure. When, however, they hear and see those messages from infancy to adulthood, their chances of making right decisions increase ten-fold. Service clubs, churches, schools and recreational programs, must move away from single-focused youth activities and begin asking the tough questions about how their programs can become a part of the consistent and persistent messages a community needs to provide its children. Our children and youth need activities, but activities need to integrate with systems that support those messages.

The minister, the teacher, the counselor, and the social worker in Charlene's life must find ways to communicate with each other throughout her development as a child. Again, single programmatic solutions contribute to the welfare of the child, but they are seldom the whole answer. Each of us can look back and identify single events or relationships that were critical to our development, but the success of those events or relationships in our lives was in large part due to the context in which they happened.

When I was ten years old, my mother and father separated briefly. My father was not in the home for approximately six months. I was his namesake and the two of us were close. I felt the pain of his abandonment and the anxiety of an uncertain future. During those six months, we seldom heard from him and he never spoke to me directly. The lot next to our house had a public utility shed with metal doors at the end of a gravel driveway. Like many young people, I collected baseball cards and would assemble all-star teams. I would organize my baseball cards into a lineup and pace off the approximate distance between the pitcher's mound and home plate. I marked on the metal doors a strike zone and used large gravel stones as a baseball. For hours, I would imagine playing in the all-star game or a World Series game, and, of course, I was always the winning pitcher - saving the game at the last moment in the last inning with the last batter. During those months, I would throw rock after rock at those doors and felt I could hear the roar of crowds for every strike I threw.

On one Sunday afternoon, I was pitching in the seventh game of the World Series: the Yankees vs. the Reds. My father had been gone for three months, and I had withdrawn into my own fantasy world. My mother, grandparents and teachers worried. A neighbor from across the street interrupted my fantasy world, with the question, "Do you play baseball with a team?" I had often watched our neighbor and his two sons pile into their station wagon with baseball equipment and head for practice. They wore ball caps with a large "O" on them with the strange emblem of the Optimists Club on the back of the cap.

Mr. Patterson had been one of those men who always watched out for the kids in the neighborhood. Kids never knew he was there, but he always seemed to appear as needed. When he asked me about playing on a team, I said, "No." I further explained that my ball glove was too old and torn and that I never had the $15 to sign up. That evening he met with my mother and mysteriously the $15 was paid. He gave me a glove to use, and handed me one of those blue and yellow ball caps with the Optimists Club insignia. He told me he would pick me up at 5:30 p.m. for ball practice.

Playing for the Optimists was more than I ever dreamed. I had a uniform, spikes, glove, and numerous adults who always asked me how I was doing. Mr. Patterson intervened at the right time. I was beginning to show signs of being in real trouble and certainly at-risk. School didn't matter anymore, and some of the neighborhood punks were enticing me into throwing more than rocks at vacant buildings. It didn't matter to Mr. Patterson or the Optimists club member, who read the Optimist creed to us once a week at practice, that I was "at-risk." What mattered to them was that I was a 10-year-old boy who, for that period in his life, needed an additional adult. I heard messages about character, God, and the importance of doing well in school.

My father came home just in time to see me play in the last four games of the season. As my father stepped back in, Mr. Patterson did not step out, but he made plenty of room for my dad. My father understood why Mr. Patterson was so important to me. Over the next three years, he never complained when I would bolt out the door towing cleats, bat, and glove to pitch for Mr. Patterson's Optimists Club team.

It was not just a baseball game. It was not just a nosy neighbor; it was not one more child caught in the middle of a marital difficulty. Mr. Patterson and the Optimists Club of Hickman Mills, Missouri understood that youth need adults and youth need activities where more than baseball is taught. The Optimists paid for the uniform, the coach was a volunteer, the community built the ballpark, and the schools provided the practice field. When there were more kids than teams, they added teams. Everyone got to play and everyone had a chance to belong. The coaches talked about the importance of schooling, honesty, fairness, and teamwork. Each group communicated with each other to create community synergy. In the midst of isolation, pain and distress, somebody reached out and the community provided a context for support and assistance.

As expressed in the preface of this work, *Mister, can you get me out of here* is a question most of us have raised, and most of us have heard. At various times in our lives, each of us has needed to ask that question. That there was somebody available, that there was a place to go and that ultimately, somebody assisted in your rescue is a credit to the support systems we built in our neighborhoods and our communities.

Dennis Archer, the former mayor of Detroit, made the argument that when Little League sports disappeared from his city, gang violence and homicides increased. The voluntary associations fled the city and the traditional rescuers gave up on the toughest of the tough. Gone were the basic institutions that bind communities to their children. Something as basic as access to spring and summer sports or afterschool programs disappears and you create a climate for trouble.

Policy Analysis

That our children continue to be pushed into the night and all we hear is their voices of despair is a testimony to a callousness and self-indulgence that has become modern America. Unfortunately, many other nations are imitating this America. In the United States, we will push one million children onto the welfare rolls this year because their voices can't vote and because communities have surrendered their power to Washington or to a State Capitol. Globally, we will watch 15 million young people seek access to education only to be denied. How we rescue our children will ultimately be the test of our strength and character as a nation and as members of a global community. Volunteers and citizens can no longer afford to wait for government to solve our problems. We must reshape our communities.

Perhaps, as we reshape our communities, we will reshape the governments we have elected to serve us. We will reshape ourselves. It is time that we create a flotilla of rescuers that will come to our shores of trouble and deliver us from indifference and from systems too complex to make an individual difference.

One of the most significant issues facing our nation is the growing disengagement and disenfranchisement of America's youth in the civic process. They volunteer at rates higher than at any other time in the history of our country. Seven out of ten volunteer on a regular basis. However, fewer of them are voting and most have become cynical about the political process. This lack of civic engagement is compounded by the fact that a significant number of youth have little or no appreciation for the basic institutions that guide and shape our nation. Whether it is the military, law enforcement, or education, increasingly those institutions seem irrelevant. The youth do not know the history of these institutions and therefore do not see value in their preservation.

The social and economic conditions of our youth and families are not improving. The new homeless population is single moms and children, challenging the resources of many of our large cities. They are replacing the single, mentally ill male sleeping on door-stoops in the downtown areas of our communities. These moms and their children are floating from shelter to shelter looking for any respite in their search for some kind of stability. This growing population of young homeless obviously faces challenges in school. They switch schools on an average of five times a year. Those who reach the age of emancipation (16 in most states) drop out and seek employment.

Nations must revisit their policy priorities. They can no longer depend on the simple good will of non-profit organizations or NGOs to pick up the pieces of a broken community. Nations can be judged by how they budget. The fact that the United States has spent nearly $800 billion on a ten-year war in Iraq while child advocates continue to fight over the scraps left over from the defense department demonstrates our government's priorities. To make things worse, most child-advocacy organizations are silent about this disparity in how we budget. The voices raised before Congress are the voices that have the largest lobbying budgets, the voices that have the greatest access because of campaign donations, and the voices of self-interest groups whose major goal is to protect their own wealth.

The situation is even worse in the developing world. Governance remains the single biggest challenge. Corruption is a way of life and dependency has become the norm. Moving institutions into action to protect, rescue, and invest in youth is largely a fiction.

We know what works here and abroad. Creating the political will to invest in our youth and children remains the challenge. Poverty, hunger, and war are all issues we know how to address. Bringing people together and developing common goals and evidence-based strategies should become the priority action.

Chapter Two - Ten Seconds in the Saddle

Okay, I admit it; I am an unabashed country western music fan. Even though I love all kinds of music, classical, hip-hop, gospel, and more, it is country, folk, and blue grass music that get to my soul. Please, no comments about the depth of my soul. I have resisted numerous musical references in this book, but I can no longer resist. Chris LeDoux on his CD, *Cowboy*, has a wonderful song about a rodeo cowboy. The chorus is very clear and summarizes a major theme of this chapter. "I would gladly take ten seconds in the saddle for a lifetime of watching from the stands." While I must confess that I have never ridden a bronco intentionally, I have been thrown from several horses in my day. I have been to numerous rodeos and have stood to my feet holding my breath while a bronco rider stayed on the mount for the mandatory ten seconds. It is thrilling to watch. On many of those occasions, I have thought or wondered to myself why an individual would do this on purpose. It is painful and dangerous. Bronco riders are risk takers. Many are risk takers on and off the rodeo circuit. The bravado in LeDoux's song asserts it is better to be in the game than to watch, better to be a player than a spectator.

Certainly, since September 11, 2001, we are summoned to engage. President Bush challenged us in his January 2002, State of the Union Address to become citizens and not spectators. Citizenship has many demands and one of them is to be involved in your community. *The virtue found in citizenship is the capacity to see a problem and then to engage the problem in a way that brings it to solution.* Citizenship does not run from the challenges of a problem, regardless of the size or the complexity. Rather citizenship requires us to *enflesh* ourselves in the midst of the quagmire. It can get messy and it certainly can be scary, but the citizen would rather be there than watching from the stands. The core compunction of a citizen is engagement. Citizens will wrestle with issues, tackle problems, confront injustice, and proclaim truth, as it needs to be proclaimed. *A citizen's greatest betrayal would be to do nothing when much would be required.* Citizenship does not ask about success or failure, it simply asks about duty and responsibility. Authentic citizenship emerges from transformational commitment. To put it more succinctly, citizenship comes from the heart or the soul and manifests itself in authentic behavior. Citizenship is one of those things that defy a complete or thorough definition, but when you see it – you know it.

Hope in these troubled times. Well now, let me be so bold as to suggest *that authentic citizenship reveals even greater power and potency when it is infused with a personal and very real dimension of faith.*

Folks, these are troubled times. During the tenth anniversary of 9/11, we were in a time of reflection where we were reminded of the murder and death of nearly 3,000 of our fellow citizens in New York, the Pentagon and in a field in Pennsylvania. Globally, thousands of children die of famine and disease in the Horn of Africa and Kenya. Human trafficking has surfaced as an issue that reminds us that human slavery is not diminishing but increasing. Drug traffickers in Mexico killed over 40,000 individuals completely destabilizing that country. Civil war and economic and political stability still capture the headlines on the continents of Africa and Asia. As horrific as these events are – there are equal tragedies facing this country and our fellow citizens throughout the world. Just to give one example - there are 40 million children in our world that are HIV positive and last year 3 million of them died. In some countries, 20% of the children, one in five, will die before the age of five. In this country, 20% of our own children will wake up hungry because of insufficient food or resources.

Let's return for a few moments back to September 11, and those troubled times. On Bruce Springsteen's CD, *The Rising*, he writes of the many firefighters who entered the battered and damaged buildings of the World Trade Center. *The sky was falling and streaked with blood – I heard you calling me then you disappeared into the dust. Up the stairs, into the fire, Up the stairs, into the fire, I need your kiss, but love and duty called you someplace higher – somewhere higher, Somewhere up the stairs, into the fire.* And the chorus: *May your strength give us strength. May your faith give us faith. May your hope give us hope – May your love give us love.*

Strength, faith, hope, and love. Love and duty call you into the fire.

This is a metaphor for us. We are called into the fire. Firmly planted in the midst of our pain, anxiety, and hurt is the cross of Jesus Christ. A cross that bore our savior where he hung spread eagle on the town garbage heap for you and for me. On one side of that cross is the message of hope and mercy and on the other side is justice and judgment. I can face his judgment because I have experienced his mercy. Because we have experienced his mercy – we are now prepared to go into the fire. We are called to be citizens, regardless of the country we live in, and citizenship pulls us into the fire. But in the fire, there is an angel of redemption with the face of God.

In the Bible, we find a compelling story in the third chapter of Daniel, King Nebuchadnezzar builds a golden idol and demands everybody worship it. Three refused - Meshach, Shadrach, and Abednego. The king built a fire seven times hotter than normal. He binds them and puts them in shackles and casts them into the fiery furnace. Verse 24 picks up the narrative: "Then King Nebuchadnezzar leaped to his feet in amazement and asked his advisers, 'Weren't there three men that we tied up and threw into the fire?' They replied, 'Certainly, O king.' He said, 'Look, I see four men walking around in the fire, unbound and unharmed, and the fourth looks like a son of the gods.'"

If we could just grasp this, then we could fully appreciate the significance of hope in times of trouble or distress. You and me, in our schools, our jobs, our homes, and regardless of the pain that we may see or know in those environments – we are called into the fire. However, once we are in the fire, someone stands with us.

Corrie ten Boom, Dutch writer who sheltered Jews escaping Nazi Germany, wrote of our Savior, "There is no pit so deep that he is not deeper still." I don't care what it is we face – what challenges beset us, what wars may threaten us, or what famine may consume us – we are summoned to engage. We cannot run and we dare not ignore the fourth person in the fire. He is there for us for all time and eternity.

The reality of his presence in the midst of the fire makes me want to engage, makes me want to find a way to spend the ten seconds in the saddle. I don't want to be a spectator when people are jumping from buildings to escape the fire, or now, have become innocents at the hands of predators that seek to destroy us.

Whatever your fear or your hurt, I am confident that the hope that is ours in Jesus Christ will transform us from observers of our culture to being participants in building a culture of redemption. In your home, with your children, with your spouse, with your employer, you can enter the fire – and your strength will give us strength, your faith will give us faith, your hope will give us hope and your love will give us love.

It Isn't Over – Until It is Finished

To fully grasp the mission to prevent poverty, hunger, crime, violence, and drug abuse in our communities, we must realize our work will never be fully completed. Each victory is replaced with another potential failure, and every failure reminds us of our need to keep finding new strategies to meet the needs of our brothers and sisters victimized by these threats to our physical, spiritual, and emotional security. I learned early on that one cannot afford to quit.

Junior high and senior high school is that wonderful time in a person's life to discover limits and potential in a whole range of areas, from athletics to academics. It took me a while to recognize that I had limited athletic ability. I was eventually to become a better than average football player with several scholarship offers, but it took great discipline and time to achieve that goal. My junior high athletic experience was anything but stellar. The football coach at Jean Baptiste Junior High School, in the Hickman Mills School District was also the track and basketball coach. If you played football, it was required that you also run track. Track was a conditioner for football and it allowed our coach to develop our speed and strength.

While the school had a no-cut policy, he was not required to play or enter you into competition unless he felt that you were qualified. Inter-scholastic competition was limited to other junior highs in the area and to travel to another school to compete was always an honor. Parents of the participating athletes provided transportation to these events. School buses, in those days, were seldom used to transport students to extra-curricular events. I soon noticed that student athletes whose parents volunteered to drive were always taken on road trips. Suddenly, I saw my opportunity to compete. I pleaded with my mother to be a permanent driver. In fact, out of six road trips in my eighth-grade year, she was able to provide transportation for only three and I only traveled to those. It was obvious, that I was there because of my mother's wheels.

On one trip to Center Junior High School, the coach said he needed a quarter-miler (440 yards). I was standing on the sidelines following the coach around in the event there might be an opportunity to compete. In practice, when I competed, I ran the 220, not the 440. That reality did not dissuade me from volunteering to be his 440 man. When I approached him and told him I could run the 440, he hesitated, then said, "Go ahead Copple, get in there." He pulled me aside and offered other advice. He pointed to one of the Center Junior High School stars and said, "All you need to do is keep up with him. If you can do that, then you have an opportunity to win."

I took my position in the fifth lane of the starting blocks. I looked up and saw Debbie Blackburn, the 8th grade love of my life standing there watching me do my stretching activities. This was my chance to impress Debbie, shock my mother and convince her that driving 20 miles with a group of juvenile boys was worth it; and to prove to my coach that I could contribute and make a difference for my team. So much was riding on this one event. What was so hard about running a quarter of a mile? I figured I could do this, and after all, how fast could this guy be? I will just keep up with him; I told my delusional self.

The starting pistol announced the beginning of the race, and I was off. I was right on the trail of John Beeson, Center Junior High School's finest. I soon fell in behind him, running with everything I had. Soon he was about ten yards ahead of me, but close enough to catch in the stretch, I thought. About the 180 mark, we turned the second corner on the track and suddenly I felt the force of a head wind. This was no ordinary head wind; this head wind could have downed a plane. It was like hitting a wall. I started fading and the other six runners passed me with little notice or fanfare. At about the 220 mark I was in a slow jog and suddenly lost my legs and my capacity to go on. Suddenly, I stopped. I began the long walk across the football field. As I approached the starting blocks, I could hear the coach asking, "Where is Copple, what happened to him?" He was standing with his hand cupped over his eyes to shade the western sun looking for his ill-suited runner. I tapped him on the shoulder and said, "Coach, I couldn't finish." He looked at me with eyes of disappointment and said, "You can't just quit a race. You should finish even if you have to walk." He couldn't have said anything worse to me.

For years, I lived with the reality that I had never finished that race and officially, I am still on the track waiting to cross the finish line. Over the years, this event has become a source of amusement to friends and family. While a humorous illustration of my own fallibility, it still bugged me that I didn't finish what I had started.

Several years ago and about 30 years after my failed attempt to beat John Beeson in the 440, I was preparing to leave Kansas and move to Washington to assume my duties as President of Community Anti-Drug Coalitions of America. My two daughters, Jamie and Jessica, were staying in Kansas, and I figured this would be my last opportunity to show them some of my growing up spots in the Kansas City area. We drove the two hours and checked into a hotel. We traveled around the city and through neighborhoods that helped define and shape my character. They had heard me tell the story of my unfinished race many times. Jamie, who was 16 at the time, turned to me and said, "Dad, where is the school where you ran that race you didn't finish?" I asked, if they wanted to see it. They said, "Sure" as if to appease me. We drove over to Center Junior High School. We got out of the car and walked down to the track. It was a Saturday and nobody was around. I stood on the track looking around, it was quiet and I was rather pensive, thinking about that spring day 30 years before. Suddenly, Jamie broke the silence with a strange suggestion. Challenging the very heart of all my parenting, she said, "Dad, you have always taught us to finish what we start, and you have often used your experience in the 440 as an example of why you should never quit." I said, "That is true and please never forget it." "Well, Dad," she said, "you have tennis shoes on, why don't you finish it?" I said with some horror and disbelief, "What?" Jessica, the eleven-year-old at the time, added, "Yeah, Dad, I will be Debbie Blackburn and cheer for you." "Come on, Dad" they pleaded, "Finish the race." They were serious, and they were giving me an opportunity to illustrate what I had preached. I said, "Okay, but I am 30 years older and several pounds heavier, if you don't mind I will start at the 220 mark across the field." They concurred, and I walked across the field to the other side.

For several minutes, I stood there looking at my daughters yelling, screaming and cheering me on. Soon I began a slow jog around the corner and began sprinting at about the 320 mark. I closed my eyes and imagined all those people in the stands who were there 30 years before. I ran faster and faster. Jamie had taken her belt off and improvised a finish tape held by both of my girls. As I ran through their belt, I held my hands up as if I was some victorious champion. They cheered and patted me on the back and praised me for my good race. We fell on to the track and laughed and laughed some more and Jamie said, "You did it… you finished the race. It's over - no more regrets Dad, you finally finished." She also chided me and said, "Now Dad, I never want to hear that story again!"

That was a great and powerful moment between a dad and his daughters. Yet, it was also a deep and profound lesson that I have since come to understand and appreciate. Seldom are things so clear as when you have finished a long and difficult task. Did finishing that race matter to anybody but me? No, but it was my event, my task and in many ways, my responsibility. There have been other things in my life that I have not finished and some tasks, while well conceived and even well designed, simply didn't merit the time and attention it takes to complete the event. Things change and the reasons for beginning them are no longer in play. It is the better part of wisdom to walk away.

There have been moments in my work with young people when I thought it would be easier to simply walk off the track and do something else with my life. Years ago, a television journalist, Diane Sawyer, asked me the rather impertinent and arrogant question, "Do you really believe that teenagers can make decisions? After all, aren't they really just bundles of emotion?" Young people bounce from one issue and concern to the other with little regard for long-term consequences. Her experience with teenagers was obviously limited, but her experience defined her bias against youth and their power to make a difference when they choose to make a difference. To be sure, working with young people is challenging and requires the patience of Job. Yet, the decisions we make when we are 14 through 35, are the decisions that are fundamental to the future direction of our lives. This period establishes the norms for how we work, how we play, how we develop relationships, how we fulfill responsibility. It is the stage when our values come into sharp focus and we move away from the arbitrary rules established by the adults in our lives. Gradually, values and decisions become ours and not simply reflexive or reactionary.

Throughout history, adults have been concerned about behavior and choices made by young people regarding their use of alcohol, tobacco and other drugs. The history of substance abuse and the reaction it has caused among people of religion, the cultural elite and, frankly, among most American families has been concern, shock and often disappointment. In a 24-hour period, riding on an airplane and traveling in a jeep to a retreat center high in the mountains of Colorado, I heard two separate stories of family tragedy related to substance abuse. A father from Oklahoma placed his 17-year-old stepson in a treatment center for marijuana use and a colleague reported his story of losing his wife and 8-year-old son in a car accident caused by a drunk driver. He has lived with that pain for 14 years. It is one of the reasons that he is so engaged in helping other young people make right choices about controlled substances.

I am an avid reader of biography, especially biographies of American Presidents. I have read biographies of Washington, Adams, Jefferson, Jackson, Grant, Wilson, the two Roosevelts, Truman, Nixon, Johnson, Kennedy, Ford, Clinton and Obama. All of them have had experience with substance abuse in their families. Several of them have lost brothers, children, and spouses to the diseases that are a consequence of addiction. The problem is pervasive and in reality, it has always been a problem in American history. Unfortunately, this same problem is defining the health and safety issues of nations throughout the world. Young people see the conflicts; they have aunts and uncles, moms, and dads who have been touched by the problem. We have yet to find a message that can counter the allure and high of illicit drugs. It is powerful stuff and the pleasure it provides is an escape from the realities that come crushing in on us in difficult moments. This reality is why the metaphor "war on drugs" is problematic. If this is a war then it is our own Vietnam with little promise or hope of digging our way out of the quagmire that continues to sink us. Yet, it is a battle that we must continue to fight.

When you attend an AA meeting or visit with individuals who are in recovery, you have the very real and clear impression that they are running a marathon measured by their daily ability to remain in recovery. The disease of addiction gnaws away at the very core of their existence. Whether they have been in recovery for two months or twenty years, it is the same and the power of the addiction is incredibly difficult to counter. The combination of will and environmental change enables them to run the race.

Those of us working in this field, and many are in recovery, arise each day to the reality that we will not solve this problem and that we will not significantly alter the landscape of the forces and influences that contribute to substance abuse, violence, poverty, or individual isolation. We will attend meetings, design new programs aimed at building community resiliency and affect policy, post signs about the dangers of drug abuse, and run television spots with the hope of changing behavior. However, the next generation will have to fight the same battle and the one after that will do the same. The strategies will vary and we will continue to recycle the strategies offering minor adjustments in program and practice. The reality is that Presidential medals are seldom awarded to this field, for this field is a reminder to the nation that we have not dealt with our addictions and the stigmas attached to them. We are conflicted and the conflict is seen in the home and in the policies that we adopt to address the issue. Moms and dads will drink and hope that their children will not. Moms and dads will smoke and tell their children that it is a nasty habit. Sixty-one percent of the baby boomer parents used drugs during the 60s, but 95% do not want their children to use them. The FDA adopts strong regulatory language to label nicotine a drug, but the U.S. Department of Agriculture subsidizes the tobacco industry. We encourage youth to participate in sports and athletic competition, but our heroes step up to the plate with "chew" firmly ensconced between their cheek and teeth. Belching frogs and sexy young people walk beaches. They glamorize the use of these substances and appeal to the imagination. Madison Avenue and their clients will continue to convince us that there is no danger to these drugs. Universities adopt policies that suggest they are going to crack down on underage drinking and drugs, but allow fraternities and sororities to host golf tournaments that allow a drink for every ball hit or permit kegs at events where underage students attend. This hypocrisy and double standard is not lost on our youth. They understand the duplicity.

The environment contributes to burnout of leadership in the field and the temptation to stop at the halfway mark of a distance race. We are bucking a cultural norm that does not surrender easily. Yet, we go on. There are reasons for this stubbornness and there are reasons why we cannot or will not be bought-out by the powers that would suggest we give up. The individuals working to address these problems are the guerrilla fighters or freedom fighters that will not let the tyranny of addiction go unchallenged. The sooner we grasp the nature and reality of our enemy, the sooner our ability to transcend its power in our lives. Regardless of the metaphor, ours is a struggle that requires us to keep our eye on the victory. We cannot fail for to fail is to surrender the future of our nation's young people.

While attending a Baltimore Orioles home baseball game at the beautifully designed Camden Yards, I was struck by my reaction to Cal Ripkin. His performance in this particular game reminded me so much of what I have come to expect of myself and my colleagues volunteering or working in this field. The Orioles were playing the Cleveland Indians. Both teams were in first place in their respective divisions. The Indians jumped off to a 4-run lead after the first inning. Nobody panicked and slowly the Orioles by the fifth inning tied Indians at 5-to-5. Cal Ripkin, in the bottom of the sixth, came to the plate and hit a resounding homerun putting the Os in the lead 6-to-5. You expect this of the Hall of Famer Cal Ripkin, but I was still amazed that he continued to do the job and he did it at just the right time. Two more runs scored and by the top of the 9th inning, the score was 8-to-5 in favor of the Orioles. The Orioles took the field and Ripkin was playing his then familiar third base. The Indians began chipping away at the relief pitcher and a line shot fired down the third base line. Ripkin committed an error and now runners crouched on first and second. The next batter came to the plate and fired another hit down the third-baseline. Ripkin made a second error allowing the bases to fill. There were two outs. I began thinking to myself, how could Ripkin do this? What inconsistency! What a time to screw up! Forget his home run; forget that two innings before he had made a sensational catch to throw the lead runner out at second base. Forget that he has played in more consecutive games than any player in the history of the game. All of that seems irrelevant in the light of two fielding errors that have loaded the bases. Cleveland's most powerful and unpredictable hitter stepped to the plate. Soon the count was full and there was but one pitch left to be thrown. The relief pitcher fired a 98-mph fastball past the swinging batter. The game was over and everyone breathed a sigh of relief. I said to the guy next to me, "Can you believe, he made two consecutive errors. Man, that is weird!" He responded, "He also hit a homerun, made a sacrifice fly scoring a runner, hit into a fielder's choice. What do you want from him, perfection?" I guess I do and I guess that is my problem. To err is human to forgive is divine. I am reminded of a bumper sticker I saw recently promoting the can-do attitude of the United States Marine Corps, "You have heard that to err is human and to forgive is divine – neither are policies of the United States Marine Corps." I like that!

Our expectations of each other in this effort are sometimes overwhelming and conflicting. In communities throughout the globe, there are heroes, much like Cal Ripkin who show up each day to play the game. They do unusual things at unusual times. They call a young person, just when the young person needs to hear from them. They invite the right leader to the right meeting and suddenly they are hooked into the cause. Critical incidences can lead to unintended consequences. People expect us to solve poverty or drug abuse overnight. They love what we do and they come and participate as spectators waiting for us to do the next miracle. Sometimes, we do it. Sometimes, we commit two consecutive errors and the very possibility of victory is threatened. Win or lose, the people I have come to know working in this field will show up at the park, dress out, and again, do their best to win.

The race may not be over and the sight of victory appears to be fading, but if we do not do it, then nobody will do it. Our children need and expect more of us than simple wishes for success. They demand the work and the work we will do. The race isn't over until we cross the finish line.

Chapter Three – The Voice of Our Vocation

Living with the end in mind is the second habit found in Stephen Covey's *Seven Habits of Highly Effective People*. Covey creates a powerful image for us when he summons us to imagine attending our own funeral as if the funeral were today. He asks us to make a list of things or statements that family and friends would say at our funeral. He then challenges us to imagine the funeral taking place five years in the future. What would we want people to say about us? The exercise is really about setting goals and creating a world of our own making. He challenges us to take responsibility for shaping and creating a world that we would be happy to celebrate. If we achieve those goals, the remarks or comments at our funeral would probably be very different. This exercise is not only about personal goals and objectives, but is applicable to organizations and program initiatives. It is an excellent tool for planning. When it is all said and done – what do we want them to say about us? More often than not, we get to those outcomes by either accident or serendipity. How do we prepare for the race? How do we prepare to engage as opposed to being spectators? How do we shape our world in such a way as to truly make a difference?

Finding our Vocation

Without a doubt, the single biggest challenge facing individuals and groups is focusing on what it is we are truly meant to do or be. We often manage by crisis where the best laid plans of individuals and organizations are delayed by what appears to be the urgent request or expectation by funder, the squeaking wheel in our community, or some influential political force. Goal setting and strategic planning documents are the most frequently developed and most frequently underutilized documents in our personal and organizational libraries. So many forces and influences divert us from our plans. This makes the pursuit of vocation or calling extremely challenging.

The word "vocation" has its root in the Latin word *vocare* – to call or summon. The implication behind the etymology of this complicated word is that the call or summons is to a specific task or opportunity, usually within the context of a religious setting. However, educators use the secular application when we refer to a certain curriculum as being vocational or technical. Further, the meaning behind vocation suggests that it is usually time limited and clear. When people review my resume or take the time to hear about my various jobs and career experiences, they are often amazed and always startled by the diversity of my background. I am not surprised. When I examine my life and career, it is clear that I have often struggled with the age-old question of what I want to be when I grow up. The truth is, that since the age of fifteen, I have had a clear sense of what I want said at the funeral. The end goal has always been the same – to serve Jesus Christ with all my heart, mind, soul and strength and that my service would be in support to others. The expression of this service has varied widely over time. Further, to be sure, how folks have viewed that goal has also fluctuated through the years.

Since the age of fifteen, my jobs have included stock boy, emergency room clerk, youth pastor, drug counselor, graduate assistant, lecturer, teacher, professor, public relations director, journalist, writer, school administrator, coalition leader, community organizer, organizational CEO, organizational COO, national spokesperson on crime, violence, and substance abuse, and now business owner with expertise in international development. In each of these experiences, with perhaps the exception of stock boy (my first job), I entered them with a sense of calling. That is – these jobs would help achieve my primary goal of service. Yet, more often than not, the transition from one position of service to another has been more by accident than design. The consequence has often been the loss of energy or focus. While diversity of activity can be interesting, diversity can also frustrate efforts to "go deep" into an issue or career. The same can be said for organizational activity. To avoid this pitfall, attention must be given to our vocation or calling. Four admonitions might be helpful.

1. Understand the source of the calling and attend to its evolving purpose

2. Develop skills to implement the calling

3. Test new challenges and opportunities against the purpose of the calling

4. Evaluate and assess the outcomes of all activities as to whether or not they advance the purpose of the vocation or calling.

The first admonition is to understand the source and evolving purpose of the summons or call. The range is from the personal to the organizational in nature. That is, as with my calling, it is very personal and contains significant spiritual and religious overtones. It has evolved over time based on education and exposure to new themes or issues within the context of the overarching goal of service. Periodically in my life, when confronted with weariness I have evaluated whether or not the overarching goal is still valid. For 45 years, it has remained constant.

On the other hand, for organizations I have worked in or helped to develop, the calling was determined by a particular issue or problem we were seeking to solve, be it substance abuse among kids, the threat of gang violence in a local community or the growing global HIV/AIDS pandemic in Africa. The source of the call or summons was a founder, a board, or a funder. Regardless, there were forces or influences that prescribed a particular mission or focus. A crisis in a community as illustrated with the rise of gang violence, or drinking under the influence that took the life of a family member – all contributed to shaping an individual or organization's mission or calling. Throughout one's tenure in an organization, it is important to question or attend to the source of the calling or summons. Is this still what you want to achieve or accomplish? The one constant and most consistent threat to organizations is mission creep or mission drift. Either way, either movement – creep or drift – is a threat. There is nothing wrong with shifting focus – the important thing is to ask periodically the question about whether or not we are still on track. Therefore, pay attention to the purpose of the calling and the clarity of the mission.

The second admonition is about being prepared to fulfill the task. Preparedness in this context is about skill development. Do we have the competencies necessary to fulfill the calling or vocation? As mentioned elsewhere, most of us did not enter the nonprofit or NGO world because we had planned on this profession since childhood. Again, my family is still trying to figure out what I do for a living. In college, I did not major in criminal justice, substance abuse prevention, international development, public health, or violence management strategies. For the most part, these majors did not exist. Yet, because of vocational choices and responding to changing needs in my community, I found myself involved in these arenas. I certainly utilized skills I had acquired as a journalist, school administrator, teacher, and public relations director. All of these were very helpful as I set about creating first a local coalition and then second, a national organization serving coalitions. Over time, I had to develop skills around policy analysis, marketing, membership development, mediation and conflict resolution, to name a few.

In the nonprofit world, we find virtue in the fact that we hire people – not positions. One CEO in the nonprofit world asserts that he embraces the Tom Landry approach to hiring staff. Landry was the longtime coach of the Super Bowl championship football team, the Dallas Cowboys. Landry hired talent and then molded them to positions. Again, there is something right about this approach, in that it focuses on innate talent. This approach, however, is not always effective. In this case, virtue does not equate with effectiveness. I am not suggesting that we scuttle virtue for effectiveness, what I am suggesting is that we give time and attention to the development of skills. We need to search for specific skills. We need to develop new skills, and we need to constantly test our current skills against the competencies necessary to fulfill our vocation.

It is also in the context of skill development that we should explore disruptive technologies. Elsewhere, we have defined disruptive technology and seen its relevance for producing community change. Yet, as agents of change in the nonprofit world and in the world of service looking for skills and approaches that stimulate change can serve as a catalyst. Innovation, not always viewed favorably by founders and funders must continue to guide our planning.

The third admonition relevant to vocation is the need to test the environment or new challenges and opportunities against the purpose of our calling or vocation. If we clearly have a sense of what it is we are supposed to do and why we are supposed to do it, then we should be able to stay focused on our mission or calling. Because nonprofits operate based on the need to acquire on-going funding to support our mission, any request for proposals (RFP), or any new project closely related to the mission or purpose of the organization becomes appealing. Living within the confines of our vocation and fulfilling our calling will be challenging if we are constantly chasing the next grant that seems within our competencies.

While working at the National Crime Prevention Council, the organization had a legitimate wrestle over whether or not we should be involved in alcohol prevention programs. We received a request to sponsor a national conference on Alcohol and Crime. The U.S. Department of Justice had recently held a summit on alcohol and crime and the links seemed obvious. However, and correctly so, the Board of Directors challenged the staff and me to demonstrate how our involvement furthered our mission of building safer and more caring communities. Alcohol issues had not been a part of the work of NCPC and they needed to know what had changed. Further, they asked, "Are there not other organizations better suited to this work?" Because of the changing demographics associated with crime, we were able to demonstrate the relevance of alcohol interventions as a crime prevention strategy. This was not about chasing the funding. This was about understanding a changing environment and if the agency was to be true to its vocation or mission, then it required them to not only understand the changing environment, but to adopt appropriate interventions to assist communities in the over consumption and illegal purchase or access to alcohol. Alcohol contributes to crime. A year later, the agency went through a strategic planning process.

Access to the instruments of lethality, including guns, drugs, and alcohol are now part of the agencies ten-year strategic plan. The mission is about building safe and caring communities. People now understand, through a consistent body of research that alcohol consumption contributes to crime.

Simply taking the time to ask the question posed by the NCPC Board of Directors forced staff to clarify their intentions and to move the agency in a direction consistent with its vocation. All too often, when we are staring at a grant award, provided an opportunity, or responding to a crisis, we can ignore the question or the test of whether this is consistent with our call or summons.

The fourth and final admonition is the need to evaluate the outcomes of our actions to assess whether they advance the call or mission. The third admonition asks the question going into the project – this last question assesses the saliency of the intervention and measures the outcome against the call. Simply put – do the outcomes indicate that we fulfilled our call?

In a previous assignment at the Pacific Institute for Research and Evaluation (PIRE), we were promoting environmental change strategies to address youth access to alcohol. The research is strong, that a public health approach, changing policies, practices, and norms, around alcohol access and consumption is more effective than implementing individual educational or treatment strategies. While we would not suggest that we stop education or treatment, we were suggesting that we get more bang for our buck, by changing policy and then enforcing policy. When retail distributors apply consistent and clear policies at the point of sale on how to check and verify identification, then a community can prevent underage youth from purchasing alcohol. This strategy is far more effective than doing one-on-one education campaigns for youngsters on the consequences of using fake IDs or trying to convince them of the potential danger to underage consumption.

At PIRE, we were often confronted with grant opportunities to provide education or awareness campaigns that reinforced the educational or individual intervention approach to alcohol prevention. The outcome of individual strategies shows little impact. However, after training liquor-law enforcement agents in West Virginia on how to enforce policy changes at the point of sale, we saw dramatic decreases in underage youth attempts to purchase alcohol. The outcome validated our mission or calling.

Call it an evaluation, a post-action review, or simply an assessment, but test your results against the call or summons. Has the ball been advanced down the field? Are we making progress toward our ultimate goal?

To summarize the issue of vocation, let me relate a story shared with me by a colleague and friend. Darryl Jones is a former President of the Maryland Fraternal Order of Police. Each year, Darryl's organization held an annual golf tournament. Darryl did not play golf but always showed up to provide, what he called the *obligatory presidential wave* as people teed off from the first green. Finally, his members purchased Darryl golf clubs and lessons so that he could do more than wave. The first year Darryl played in the tournament, he teamed up with legendary golf champion Sam Snead. Mr. Snead was the celebrity pro for the tournament. Darryl stepped up to the tee with confidence, took the obligatory practice swing, lined up on the ball, pulled his club back and leveled a mighty swing. Unfortunately, he topped the ball and it rolled about twenty yards off the tee. He was angry and embarrassed. He threw his club into the bag and cart and proceeded off the tee box. Snead looked at Darryl and asked him, what to Darryl seemed like a stupid question, "Darryl, what is the objective of golf?" Darryl was in no mood for stupid questions, but out of respect for this elderly legend, Darryl said, "Well Sam, the goal of golf is to get the ball into the hole with the fewest number of strokes." Snead looked at Darryl and said, "Well that's the problem Darryl, you don't understand the goal of golf." Darryl looked at Snead and said, "Well then enlighten me, Sam, because that is what I thought we were suppose to do out here." Snead smiled and told Darryl, "the goal of golf is to advance the ball." He then asked Darryl, "Did you advance the ball with that swing?" Darryl got the point. He had in fact advanced the ball. It may not have been as far or as long as he might have hoped, but he did indeed advance the ball.

The test of our efforts is whether we truly embrace the call or summons given to us to advance our mission. Do we have the skills and do we know how to constantly test our call against new and tempting opportunities and challenges?

The assessment of your commitments, your work and your vocation, is best realized when engaged in the problem you are seeking to solve. Ten seconds in the saddle are better than a lifetime in the stands. The voices that call us from the night demand or require presence. We cannot bring rescue, health, or help from the distant world of the academy or from internal reflections of what "ought" to be done. It requires action and engagement; it requires "enfleshment" in the issue being addressed. It will be risky and the horse will throw you, but you will be the better for it - and the cause you are serving will be advanced by your commitment to stay in the saddle.

Chapter Four - To Plant and To Replant - That Is Our Mission

Years ago when I traveled from Seattle to Boston, I made a scheduled stop to visit friends in western Kansas. They pastored a church in Garden City, located in the southwestern corner of the flat and barren High Plains state. The sky is wide-open and the fields of wheat go on for miles and miles. Horizons are distant lines that fade in distinction between land and sky. There is a beauty to its isolation and you discover why there is such enthusiasm for the blooming of a wild flower or delight in the deep golden browns of a field of milo. Grain elevators rise up like medieval cathedrals, the center of community activity and commerce. Farms in this part of the world are dry-land farms averaging five to seven thousand acres in size. It takes a lot of dry-land wheat to support a single family.

On my first visit to Garden City in November of 1980, I met a farmer, who planted approximately 10,000 acres of dry-land wheat. After visiting with him for several hours and learning the challenges of his profession and the dramatic effects of President Carter's grain embargo on the price structure of wheat, he invited me to come back in June to help him with the harvest. I accepted his invitation. He put me to work driving wheat trucks, and eventually I had the honor of actually being able to guide the combine through the crowded furrows of thousands of acres of wheat ready for harvest. Large combines with 36-foot headers (that big round turning thing that captures the stalks of wheat) dotted the horizon as farmers moved hurriedly through the fields before the next storm. The days were long and families worked from sunrise to 1:00 or 2:00 in the morning to see that the harvest was in.

There was little time for rest and the work was only interrupted by one of Arlene Algrim's famous harvest lunches, served around 2:00 or 3:00 in the afternoon. She would pull a camper on the back of a pickup truck out onto the field where we worked. Soon the signal would come and all things stopped as we made our way to the daily feast that provided the bright spot in the day.

At one of those meals, I asked Clifton Algrim, the family patriarch, who possessed a deep religious faith integrated throughout his life, what he did when it hailed? He gave me a quizzical look, reserved only for the "outlander" from Boston, and said, "Let me tell you a story." When he first took over the farm in the early 50s, his father admonished him never to cut wheat on Sundays in respect to God and out of respect for the Church. "The first year I was in harvest, I shut down the combines at 11:59 p.m. on Saturday evening," he said. "You could hear the combines of my neighbors. They kept cutting well into Sunday morning. At about two in the morning," Clifton explained, "The hail came and it came. Farms around mine were affected. Complete fields were destroyed, but not one acre of mine was touched." Oh boy, I thought, I am going to get one of those stories, where because of his faith, God protected him and all others had to suffer.

The next year, the same thing happened, according to Clifton. His fields were spared and his neighbor's fields were destroyed. I looked up at him, and said, "That is amazing Clifton. How do you explain that?" "Well I am not sure," he answered. "The third year, on a Saturday evening, the storm clouds continued to threaten us with those icy pellets that fall from the sky. Everyone kept saying it was going to hail. At midnight, I cut the engines, got out of my combine and walked slowly to my pickup. I could feel the storm. Others were moving through their fields in a panic. I drove back to the house," he continued to explain, "but soon I could hear the hail begin pounding on the top of the truck. I got home, went upstairs to bed." With his aged and tanned face, Clifton looked at me, almost with a sadness, and said, "The next morning, I looked out the window, and saw my fields beaten down by the storm. The heads of wheat stalks were destroyed by the pounding of the hail." He said rather abruptly, "I had lost everything. Everything gone." I was somewhat shocked by his candor and this revelation that appeared to defy his simple faith explanations. "What did that teach you Clifton," I asked. "Teach me?" He responded, "Whether you cut wheat on Sunday or you don't cut wheat on Sunday, it will sometimes hail. It has nothing to do with whether I stop cutting at midnight or not. It just simply does not matter to nature." Given his response, I was surprised that Clifton continued to not cut on Sundays. I asked him why he continued this practice. "Because I still want to honor God with my service."

Perhaps more perplexing to Clifton was my next question. "What do you do Clifton, when you are hailed out?" He looked at me and said with both firmness and empathy, "Why, I replant." Suddenly, he yelled in that wonderful firm voice, "Let's get back to work, before this outlander brings on a storm."

"I replant." Those words have haunted me for years. They have been both a source of inspiration and a source of courage. Whenever, I feel I have been absolutely dumped on because of who I am and what I do, I think of Clifton and I think of the need and the necessity to replant. Whether in the barren farmlands of southwestern Kansas or the inner city of Boston, people in crisis display a resiliency that defies easy explanations. We best see that resiliency when there is a vivid contrast between one's potential and one's predicament. Nature, like certain forms of poverty and despair, is not predictable. You do not plan for its consequences, nor can you fully grasp the depth and significance of its impact. There is no single person or thing to blame. It is simply there and it is our challenge to navigate through its consequences. When you add into the mix poverty and despair, addiction and the apparent violence of many of our cities, you have forces that are completely out of control. Drug abuse cuts a swath of destruction and despair in the lives of its victims. All of us pay for it, regardless of our preparations, our religious tradition, or the security of our wealth.

Poverty knows no boundaries. It often appears arbitrary, not solely defined by class or geography. I have seen a poverty of the spirit that is as destructive as a poverty derived from famine. In the midst of those environments, I have witnessed courageous and bold actions that have transformed communities. Brian Odour, a young Kenyan leader is one such example. He was 19 years old when I first met him in the Korogocho slums of Nairobi. His father died from AIDS, his brother, sister, and mother are HIV positive. Yet from the rubble of his circumstances, he has emerged. St. John's Catholic church found Brian, encouraged him, supported his secondary education and now he is preparing to be a medical doctor at Kenyatta University. He took his reality and replanted his life in the heart of a soil that had more promise. Now, he is using his incredible talent, skill, and determination.

When I meet with communities, I find individuals, organizations and neighborhoods prepared to replant. Around them are despair and hopelessness of people and institutions that have tried and tried again to make a difference. Yet, they do not quit. We find resiliency in individuals and organizations to be very similar.

Resiliency is critical to our future as individuals and as communities. Resilient youth generally have five characteristics. The first is **HOPE**. A child or community that possesses hope and/or faith, daring to dream about the future and attempting the impossible, will resist falling into the trap of despair and pain. I see this everywhere, but most often in my work in Africa. In squalid Nairobi slums, children move with energy, determination, and humor. Children have a sense that there is a tomorrow and that their tomorrows possesses meaning. These children are more likely to resist drug abuse, chancy sexual behavior, and other risky behavior. Hope can be translated into faith, purpose, direction or meaning. Our world's youth have historically possessed hope and we must again, rekindle its flame in our families, schools, places of worship and renew their summons to civic and community life. For many of our children, poverty, hunger, drug abuse and the absence of a caring community have driven them into behaviors that are self-destructive and destructive to communities. We cannot afford the allure and dangers poverty or its progeny of drug abuse, disease, and isolation to destroy our children or their hope.

A second component of resiliency is **ALTRUISM**. Children and communities who recognize the need to give something away and to place themselves in the place or situation of another have greater capacity to resist the destructive and harmful elements of a community or neighborhood. We cannot afford to constantly ask what our deficits are - but now must look at our assets and figure new ways to communicate and share those assets. To be sure, our world is facing and experiencing many challenges. We should afford our children every opportunity to participate in the solutions. They have much to give and in their giving, we develop citizens who become powerful forces in the eradication of drug abuse. No program, federal, state, or local should be planned, funded or implemented without the direct and constructive participation of youth. Their capacity to volunteer and to make a difference is the seed of future volunteerism and change.

In the Lunga Lunga slums of Nairobi, my friend Nick leads a group of 40 youth volunteers. Each week these young men and women gather to collect the trash, garbage, and waste from corrugated tin houses and they move the refuse to a central collecting area. They wade into the rubble in boots and protective clothing to recycle the glass, plastics, and paper that could be used for other purposes. When I asked Nick why he was so engaged in this project - his answer was simple: "This is my community and we must do all we can to keep it safe and healthy." No great financial reward for his work, no awards or recognition - he sees his role as fulfilling a civic duty.

The third factor is to have an **INTERNAL LOCUS OF CONTROL**. When I lived in Wichita and rode with the Police Department gang unit, we entered a crack house one evening with a search warrant. We learned that the house possessed at least nine firearms and significant amounts of crack cocaine. We knew that there was at least one young child in the house. After entering the house on a no-knock warrant, we approached a bedroom with a locked door. On the door was a sign that read, "Read the Damn sign - Keep the drugs and alcohol out of my room." As we slowly opened the door, we saw an eleven year-old hiding in the corner. On the wall were posters with messages about drug-free lifestyles and a workbook given to her by a teacher about the dangers of drugs. In that same house, that child lost a parent who was arrested for possession with intent to sell over $30,000 in crack. Two weeks later, her grandmother was killed in a drive-by shooting and eventually the young lady ended up in foster care. She graduated from high school last spring with an intention to teach. Her locus of control was limited to her room - but she took a stand and demanded respect for her stand. Supported and reinforced by her community, she is now pursuing a career that will make her a contributor.

Youth voice is critical to youth empowerment. We must avoid the temptation to clichés or relegation of youth engagement to sentimental acts of participation. Their voice must be heard in the way we design, the way we promote a project, and the way we recruit youth to engage. If they are to be part of the solution, then we must find ways for them to have control of the outcomes.

ADULT BONDING is the fourth element. Any community that provides opportunities for bonding and cohesiveness with significant adults has a far greater chance of succeeding. Programs that connect children to adults and foster sustained relationships have a greater chance of contributing to the resiliency of our community's youth. When you press young people about their heroes and their role models, they seldom pull up the names of athletes, politicians, or entertainers. Rather, they usually name a parent, a grandparent, a teacher, a pastor, rabbi or mullah. Facilitating opportunities for these connections will make the difference in our attempts to rescue and our attempts to empower.

The fifth and final resiliency is the **ACQUISITION OF SKILLS**. A child, affirmed and recognized for making a sustained contribution, through music, academics, sports, or community service, feels the recognition of the host community. Communities are the same way. When neighborhoods, schools, or specific and targeted areas feel that they contribute to the whole community's effort to solve their drug and violence problems, then that community is more likely to draw a line in the sand and demand that their environments be drug and violence free.

Our offensive must strike at the nerve of poverty and its potential victims. When communities build on these characteristics or resiliencies, then there is power in their capacity to replant. They may have seen elements of their lives destroyed or beaten, but there is a foundation for continued growth and development. Replanting requires recognition that we are not simply victims of our environments or of failed policy. We are not reeds blown about in the capricious political winds of our leaders. Rather, we will rise in the morning and find a way to place the plow to the ground and seed to the furrow. We will nurture the land and we will prepare for our own harvest. We have no choice but to go on and going on is what I continue to see in communities throughout the world. While they may look and act like devastated and ruined environments, there is someone or a group of someones who are looking for opportunities to replant.

As with harvest or seasons, communities seem to live and work in cycles. Failure to realize this can often lead to despair. If you think in a linear fashion believing that one thing connects to the next and eventually we will get to the end of the problem, then we can expect always to be disappointed. Further, you cannot always anticipate the forces of change that affect communities. Community change is often the result of critical incidences that hit a neighborhood or community. An election, a shooting, a car wrapped around a tree by a teenager's drunken stupor or simple outrage over crack dealers penetrating a neighborhood, all reflect change that is unpredictable. These incidents can serve to break or motivate a community. Yet, change seldom happens without them. These events seldom entirely break citizens, but they can serve to fuel the flames of despair and thus lead to periods of inactivity. People become numb and see these events as simply another indication that everything is going to hell in a hand-basket. Then suddenly out of nowhere, somebody or something happens that sparks neighborhood and community revival and renewal. People engage.

After developing a strategic plan for graffiti removal and working with city and county agencies, we could get no real community buy-in to support our efforts. There was agreement that it was becoming a significant problem and that it certainly was becoming an eyesore. Minor efforts to remove graffiti were met by gang members' hostility and resolve to continue staking out their turf with messages of hate and revenge. After months of getting no real community buy-in to address this problem, a businessman was shot while attempting to paint over a recent "tag" by a neighborhood gang. The community leader provided a vital source of inspiration to many young people in the neighborhood. People were stunned.

The neighborhood and the violence prevention coalition seized this experience (critical incident) as an opportunity to educate the broader public on the danger of allowing graffiti to go up without a community response. Soon organized volunteer paint-outs brought together the resources of public and private sector organizations to take down the graffiti and adopt policies that all graffiti would be removed within 48 hours of it going up. Within a year, after five volunteer paint-outs, adopting a city ordinance requiring the removal of graffiti, increasing the penalties for posting graffiti, and utilizing juvenile probationers as workers to remove graffiti, the city has become virtually graffiti-free. It was all in the strategic plan, but the plan had no context in the hearts and minds of the community. When they were ready, however, after the critical incident, they had a road map for community action and community change. They were "hailed on" and then took steps to replant.

There is a season for every initiative. As organizers and volunteers, we can become frustrated by the failure of leaders and neighbors to grasp the significance of our great ideas. Prevention is the most cost-effective underutilized tool in our community arsenal. Prevention seldom reminds us of the crises around us. It is the siren reminding us of impending danger, but the danger is seldom feels real until it is in our family or in our neighborhood. That is why it is vital that we remember that the crisis and the remedy are cyclical. Things eventually come around. By our planning and thinking through solutions to specific problems and challenges faced by the community, we set a context for action when action is required. We create the community "readiness" for change.

As with my friend Clifton, he plows his ground in late summer, plants his seed in the fall, cultivates when the ground is dry and fertilizes in the spring. By June, he has a crop to harvest. He readies the soil for the eventual harvest. Sometimes it hails and he begins the process all over again. Yet, he prepares for all the contingencies. He is not destroyed by the critical incident; he often will utilize it to his advantage. There is a season for planning, there is a season for resource development and there is a season for community implementation. Implementation before the community is ready is doing your project "to" the community. Forcing projects and then inviting the community to participate in the spirit of doing it "for" the community will not create sustainability. You are a partner with the elements of your environment. You must utilize them and cooperate "with" them in order to achieve the objective. This is an endless process of creating community readiness for change.

I remember my friend Clifton complaining about a particular field overgrown with weeds. "The harvest would be difficult," he complained. Separating the wheat from the chaff is one thing, but having weeds caught up in the combine could damage equipment and it weakened the crop. A healthy field could yield as much as 50 bushels of wheat per acre. A field covered in weeds would yield as low as 19 or 20 bushels an acre. The weeds, if allowed to grow, sapped precious resources from the wheat crop. They took water, nutrients and essentially depleted the soil or environment in which the wheat grew.

In community, we have to be mindful of the weeds that can ruin our environment for youth development and community change. The field has to be cultivated and occasionally we have to do some serious weeding. The weeds include poverty, hunger, homelessness, and tolerance for an environment where vacant buildings and abandoned properties become hubs for drug dealers and gang activity. Little or no attention is given to the basic infrastructure needs of citizens. Children ride buses to schools miles away from their neighborhood and even churches, long an institution in preserving neighborhoods become commuter churches with parishioners having no attachment to their immediate surroundings. These realities sap the strength and character out of its citizens. They represent the consequences of failing to give real and immediate attention to the small things in the field of community policing.

George Knelling, James Q. Wilson and Katherine Coles have stressed the importance of attending to the small things before they become major issues that require significant resources and energy.[2] Their fixing broken windows strategy, attending to the outward signs of community decay before they become the source of high crime, where predators

---

[2]George Knelling and Katherine Coles, <u>Fixing Broken Windows,</u>

feed off the vulnerability of the population, has become a model for community policing. To be more specific, when a citizen drives through a neighborhood and they see a broken window in a building, they assume, after a brief period of time, that nobody is really in charge of that property. After a while, the buildings around that property become vulnerable and graffiti begins to appear and citizens no longer feel safe in the environment. These are the community weeds that can destroy a community's potential.

The same principle applies to the human service field. Neighborhoods with high incidents of drop-outs, teenage pregnancy, juvenile crime, and HIV/AIDS become environments for more serious index crime, poor health, and violence. If we do not attend to the first signs of environmental weeds, then we better prepare for the weeds to take over the field. The tragedy of this metamorphism that weeds choke, starve and eventually weaken the seed. It takes diligence on the part of the farmer; it takes resources and time to prevent weeds from consuming the field. As activists working with neighborhoods and schools, we are compelled to protect and preserve our communities. Attention must be given to the early signs of neighborhood decay that can ultimately threaten the whole community.

All of us have seen neighborhoods and schools where the broken window theory applied. Small things at first and then a few larger infractions, then suddenly residents and students lose confidence in the ability of those in charge to fix the situation. Nobody takes responsibility. Eventually things get out of control and all of the resources are directed toward the big problems. Had they paid attention to the early infractions, the small things, when there was time, resources and energy to control the situation, they could have made a difference. Now the situation requires a radical intervention, an intervention that is far more costly.

Yet, even in the midst of decay and hopelessness, there is always the opportunity to replant. No amount of environmental despair or community decay can ultimately thwart the human spirit, particularly when it is ready to mobilize. The recent models of community policing have provided us some useful lessons. Entire neighborhoods have become engaged in restoring and preserving order. They have taken back their parks, removed the graffiti, cleaned up their streets, fixed their broken windows and given attention to the small things that create fear among their residents. Panhandling, homelessness, or petty crime, nothing was too small to fix. When these things are fixed, the more serious index crimes diminish. Substance abuse and violence prevention workers need to give attention to this model and its ramifications for our community actions.

In collaboration with schools and social service agencies, we need to begin looking for those indicators of broken windows in our field. In those neighborhoods where the conditions have become more significantly impaired, we need to replant. We must take control block by block. This may not be easy and at first; our steps toward improvement will appear to be marginal. It is essential, however, that we do the weeding. Hail may come, but the situation is never so grave, that we cannot replant. As long as individuals are engaged, regardless of the number, there is always hope. We must find it, cultivate it grow more of it. Like a well-preserved and well-tended farm, hope is the nutrient most important to a healthy community.

Applying the Lessons

1. Hail will come! You know the axiom; no good work will go unpunished. As long as I have worked in this field, I can always anticipate that my good actions will be met by cynicism, despair and those ugly words, "I told you so." Somebody seems to always dump on my good thinking and plans. It is a fact. While for many,

this may drive them to pessimism and despair, it has for me become a reality that must be managed. It will not kill me nor will it destroy my plans. Clifton was right to look at me quizzically and think I was some kind of fool for asking what he did when it hailed. Of course, he would replant. Weather happens!

2. Implement with patience: Continuing with our metaphor of the harvest, it is important to remember that the ground was prepared in August and the harvest didn't take place until June. In between, significant activity prepared the ground to produce a crop to harvest. Plowing, planting, fertilizing, cultivating, and watering all play a role. We must implement the initiatives we put into place to rescue, to empower, and to strengthen youth with patience over time. It requires planning, resource assessment, honest evaluation of the environment and conditions facing a child at risk. It demands that we design interventions in collaboration with the young people involved. That at times, we must include their parents or guardians.

Chapter Five - Naming and Claiming Our Children and Communities

With a loud and forceful crash, a contingent of officers from the Wichita Police Department and the Sedgwick County (Kansas) Sheriff Office kicked the door in and yelled, "Police! Everybody down!" I was the ninth person of our search warrant party to enter the cluttered living room of this known crack house. It was 11:00 PM. Throughout the evening, the police had observed drug buys at the address and waited for the right time to enter and search for the valuable, but deadly crack cocaine produced by the tenants of this dark and trash-strewn home.

As I entered, the screaming of young voices from the upstairs bedroom alerted me to the presence of frightened children. As soon as the police announced that all rooms had been secured, I made my way up the stairs and entered the small room with mattresses stacked on the floor. Clothing was tossed about the room - some dirty and some clean. The smell of urine permeated the air everywhere. A fluorescent light kept going on and off, adding a surreal cast to what was clearly a nightmare for the young children. They stared at me in fear and bewilderment. Fifteen small faces looked lost in the scene being played out in their home.

The police had seen it a hundred times before. I too had seen it, but never before had I been struck by the paradox of what I was about to encounter. In the rooms below, the police began their meticulous search of the premises. They questioned the adolescents and adults who allegedly had been dealing drugs, guns and were clearly involved in human trafficking. Meanwhile, upstairs, I watched as one lone officer began assuring the children that all would be okay. This armed officer, who moments before came storming into their house, was now engaging the children in light and silly conversation. Soon, the assuring voice of the SCAT (Special Community Action Team) officer calmed their fears. As with most children, tears were easily turned to laughter by the attentive hand and their despair became, for a time at least, curiosity about the officer and the other strange observer in the room.

They asked me questions and then I asked them what schools they attended. The oldest was a third-grader; the youngest was three. The school-aged children voiced pride in their schools and wanted very much to impress the young officer and me with their accomplishments. While the children talked a mile a minute, I could hear the officers downstairs informing the occupants that they had just found thousands of dollars of crack cocaine in the basement. They offered no denial or protest because they knew they had been busted.

As I turned my attention back to the children to see if they could possibly hear or understand the conversations below, I felt a pull on my pant leg. It was a familiar pull. It was a pull I had felt a hundred times before from my own children. I looked down to see a four-year-old boldly declare in the midst of the chaos and noise, "I can write my name! Do you want to see it?"

Frankly, I was so angry at the action of this child's parents that I was in no mood to observe an exercise in penmanship. But the young officer, being much wiser than this aging educator, seized the opportunity to keep this child and her siblings occupied. "Yes," he said, "I want to see it." The youngster responded that she had paper but no pen or pencil. The officer quickly reached into his shirt pocket and handed her his gold Cross pen. *Why not a pencil?* I was thinking. *He gave her his best pen!*

Immediately, she set about the task of writing, stopping only once to show us that she could also write the number four. She wrote the number backwards, but with a twist of the paper, it became the number four. Within moments, she produced her name and together, we celebrated her accomplishment.

Moments later, I made my way back downstairs and entered other rooms of the crack house. There I saw symbols of family togetherness and efforts to do the right thing: G.E.D. exam books, correspondence course materials, and letters from friends and acquaintances. Family albums opened to pictures of aunts and uncles testified to happier days. In many ways, it all seemed so normal.

But throughout the house, there were also the cigarette lighters, the glass tubes for processing the cocaine, and the tiny sacks containing the small rocks of crack. As I observed the collection of evidence and stared into the faces of the adults who had made the crack and who were willing to sell it, I wanted to scream, "Upstairs there is a child who is celebrating the writing of her name. Does anybody know? Does anybody care?"

A child can write her name. Thousands of children arrive at that milestone daily. In the scheme of life, it is only a small thing, why should I be so upset? It is because the tragedy in our society today is that nobody notices the small steps or the small victories. Our community's pre-occupation with crime, drugs, violence, and human trafficking leaves the children as casualties. They pull at our pant leg with words of hope and we ignore them and because of our indifference we damn them to repeat the tragedies of their parents' lives.

What will happen to this child and what hope will she have if we continue to act as if she does not matter? She does matter. In the dark scene of a crack house, I heard in her insistent voice the declaration, "I will write my name and somewhere, sometime, you will notice it."

We will determine if we notice that name boldly inscribed on a high school and college diploma or written below the mug-shot pictures found in the booking documents of law-enforcement agencies or on a court docket. As a community, we must be about the task of placing that name on the diploma or it will cost us in wasted resources and in lost lives.

For some reason, that four-year-old's persistence that I see her write her name provides hope for me. We dare not ignore that hope. Jane Addams, the founder of Hull House, and an advocate for children, wrote in 1879, "[I]nfancy is the Messiah sent again and again into the arms of man to rescue him from this fallen and despondent condition; childhood comes in the fresh young radiance of hope. The thoughts of the child first beginning to think and to exist are overtold of what may be, and thus counteract the social spasm overfull of what is, they deluge the world with hope and wonder infinite in measure."

That night a child taught me a lesson. Recent national surveys and local observations would suggest that we are losing these children. Our nation's crime statistics, while down have diverted our attention from the need to create meaningful play, work, and education for many of our children. This child and thousands of her peers demand our resources, our attention, and our time. Fighting the war that creates their despair and hopelessness requires will and persistence. The conditions that cause their suffering cannot be easily fixed. We will be tempted to look for solutions that are highly visible and easily measured. If we yield to that temptation, we will have created an illusion that portends a disaster.

We need to begin now asking policymakers, volunteers, community social-service agencies, churches, and our neighbors to feel the pull of the pants leg and respond in a measured and thorough manner. Our children's survival and our future depend on the type of response we offer.

We should all want to work where we can hear the children boldly proclaim, "I can write my name." We need individuals to create a community in which that name is recognized for its goodness and promise, not its despair and hopelessness.

The story of this young lady, while specific to a crack house and a neighborhood disproportionately affected by crime, violence, and drug abuse, is a story that can be found in nearly all of America's communities. It is also a global predicament. Whether these children are victims of substance-abusing parents, crime-infested neighborhoods, or exposed to domestic and community violence, they are children that share issues across the demographic spectrum of a global culture. Most are born into poverty, most are living in a home with a single parent, and many have fathers or brothers in the criminal justice system - our euphemism for jail. The fifteen children found in that Wichita crack house are consumers and victims of a variety of systems that have both offered some relief and yet, have ultimately failed them. Food Stamps, Medicaid, crisis intervention counseling, job training, have all contributed to the survival of those fifteen youngsters. They attend schools where the per capita expenditure per student is nearly half of what is spent on each child in the most affluent section of the community.

The reality is that in the United States, over 2 million children are living on less than $2 a day. Poverty rates in many of our southern states are bordering on 20% and in Mississippi, they are at 30%. This is worse than many countries in sub-Saharan Africa.

According to a recent editorial in the New York Times by Peter Hotez, "Outbreaks of dengue fever, a mosquito-transmitted viral infection that is endemic to Mexico and Central America, have been reported in South Texas. Then there is *cysticercosis*, a parasitic infection caused by a larval pork tapeworm that leads to seizures and epilepsy; *toxocariasis*, another parasitic infection that causes asthma and neurological problems; *cutaneous leishmaniasis*, a disfiguring skin infection transmitted by sand flies; and murine typhus, a bacterial infection transmitted by fleas and often linked to rodent infestations." (*New York Times,* Sunday, August 19, 2012)

The poverty rates and the rise of infectious diseases among the poor, particularly among African-Americans and Hispanics, contribute to delayed intellectual and emotional development. These systemic issues continue to plague the global community and are now becoming realities in the most developed country in the history of modern civilization.

The four-year-old celebrating a skill that is taken for granted by the rest of us learned that skill in a Head Start classroom. Her teacher, Mrs. Doreen Kennedy, engaged Claudia in the exercise of penmanship and sat alongside her watching as she carefully scratched out each letter to form her name. Mrs. Kennedy offered suggestions and made minor corrections over the course of several days until Claudia had mastered the important but complex early skill. Now, late Saturday night in her home, she wanted to show two strangers the magic of connecting seven letters that would announce her identity. A child in an urban ghetto whose weekends were spent dodging the violence of her neighborhood and home begins forming letters taught her by a teacher. A teacher whose daily commitment to children demands that she spends time with each and every one of them to form letters and to cross a linguistic hurdle that takes a concept and gives it an image that is recognized by all of us - a name..

What's the big deal you ask? It happens every day in America and it happened to all of us at some point in our childhood. What is lost is the magic surrounding so important an event. Names are important and they are a moniker pointing to both our past and our hope for the future. The mere mention of some names will bring a variety of reactions whether it is Mister Rogers, Princess Diana, Timothy McVeigh, Adolph Hitler, Osama bin Laden, Martin Luther King, Marilyn Monroe, Mother Theresa, Barak Obama, or George Washington. All names generate some reaction.

When my grandmother (97-years-old) calls me Jimmy, I still feel her warmth, smell the aroma of her kitchen and remember the encouragement she offered in difficult times and situations. I will never forget the first time I heard the President of the United States mention my name in a speech. I was stunned and caught off guard that the most powerful man on earth, would, at one moment in time utter my name -

the name of a community organizer and teacher from Wichita, Kansas. To this day, when I have published an article or have been interviewed by the media, I will read the article and search for my name and still feel a shot of adrenaline when I see it in print.

In June 1997, I was invited to the White House to watch President Clinton sign the Drug-Free Communities Act into law. I had been the principal architect of the legislation and now was seeing the culmination of months of work and organizing. I sat in the front row and I watched the President take many pens and begin writing his name on to the legislation. As he formed each letter, I remembered Claudia and the skill required to write a name. The president's signature promised much. With his signature, he had declared my work law and now communities across the nation would benefit from the resources generated by this legislation. Programs and policies would be changed and individuals would benefit from services that would prevent them from abusing drugs, alcohol, and, tobacco.

The challenge we face in a society whose social capital seems to be waning and whose commitment to basic relationships that encourage growth and hope is that we dare not forget that we are connected. In a culture that has elevated individualism to mythological proportions, we completely forget social and communal networks have defined us for centuries. Robert D. Putnam, the most recent champion of social capital, has written in *Bowling Alone: The Collapse and Revival of American Community,* that social capital "constitutes a kind of sociological superglue." (*See footnote 2*) He further defines social capital in the following manner: "Whereas physical capital refers to physical objects and human capital refers to properties of individuals, social capital refers to connections among individuals - social networks and the norms of reciprocity and trustworthiness that arise from them."

In the context of naming and claiming our children in communities, particular attention needs to be drawn to the networks and norms that foster reciprocity and trustworthiness. In the historic Judeo-Christian world of American politics, a system of government created with checks and balances to check the avarice and vice of people, it is often difficult for us to see the culture as a place that spawns reciprocity and trustworthiness. But the reality of American history is that we are not isolated individuals operating in spatial vacuums. Our connections are deep and they are profound and those connections often bring out the best in civic and community action. I suggest that we are connected in a variety of ways and when we give attention to these connections, we can develop policies and programs that enhance our work.

Lest we believe that this need for connection is

limited to western culture or specifically, the United States, we need to be reminded that globally, children suffer from the same isolation and abandonment that contributes to their lack of development and safety. Having worked internationally for the past eight years, I am convinced more than ever that children are resilient and have an enormous capacity for change and shifting attachments. Walking through the slums of Nairobi or the make-shift streets of the Dadaab refugee camp near the Somali border, I observe children run, play, and seek attention. Yet underneath the veneer of happy faces and playful antics, you soon learn there has been enormous pain caused mostly by the irresponsibility of the adults in their world.

Global poverty, disease, and famine seem to so many of us to be an intractable problem and it is easy for us to dismiss its relevance to our lives. It is so far away and it is fraught with complex political, economic, and governance issues. We think, *I cannot do anything - therefore, I will pay no attention.* I was overwhelmed recently when I engaged in a conversation with a CARE International leader working in the Dadaab refugee camp.

This is not my story but the story of a caseworker for CARE International. It begins in Somalia and its ending is yet to be written. I found the story in the harsh and desperate world of a refugee camp in

Kenya, just 30 miles from the border with Somalia, an area controlled by Al Shabaab, the terrorist organization affiliated with Al Qaeda.

On a conference call to discuss the desperate need for grief counselors in the refugee camp, where there is one counselor for every 50,000 people, I asked a rather naive question of Michael, the CARE employee, "Just how bad is it really for the children?"

He paused and then said, "Let me tell you about Omar." He had arrived in the camp ten days before he appeared at the CARE clinic located in the IFO expansion camp. His young mother whose face and complexion added thirty years to her appearance accompanied him. In front of Omar, she told a horror story not, unfortunately, uncommon among the recent refugees fleeing into Kenya. Her homestead had been raided by Al Shabaab and all the men were tortured and killed, including her husband. They warned the women they would be back in several days to confiscate all food items. Omar's mother was terrified and feared for her own life.

On the day they arrived, Omar's mother, with his help buried herself deep in the sand and used a hollow reed she inserted into her mouth in order to breathe. She instructed Omar to give the terrorists whatever they wanted but not to reveal her hiding place. The men stopped 10 feet away from her hiding place. She could hear the exchange. They asked Omar for the location of his mother. He told them she had already left the homestead and was headed for Kenya. They knew it was a lie. They beat him and asked again. Torture and threats were not changing Omar's story. His mother was gone, he shouted.

Finally, the leader changed tactics. He offered Omar a cup of water and a biscuit. After a long silence, Omar silently pointed to the burial shelter of his mother. The leader gave him his water and the biscuit. The four terrorists dug Omar's mother out of her hiding place and gang raped her. When they finished, she found Omar sitting near a bush dividing up the biscuit - a piece for his sister, two pieces for his mother, and one for himself. Since that day, he has said nothing and has turned his rage and silence against his mother and sister.

Michael repeated, "For a cup of water and a biscuit a starving child chooses to surrender his mother to the men that killed his father." What can we expect? Michael was angry and asked, "How many counselors can you get me and do you have people that can train counselors?"

The answer to Michael's question is yes. Through African Nazarene University, we can do both. We began organizing and soon there will be volunteer counselors in place to help. Gender-based violence is a major crisis in the camps where *crisis* is the understatement of the year. Women are continually under threat. Children are in horrific pain.

The voice of Omar is one of despair and the international community seeks solutions that would alter his reality. They will make counselors available, provide education in the camp, feed him at least one hot meal a day and all of this will point to the act of rescue. The unknown of Omar's future is what he will do with this decision and how will he manage the consequences of the choice he made that day. The emotional scar tissue will forever be a reminder that in so many ways, he failed. He was a victim of adults behaving badly. If the history of oppression and abuse offer us any lessons, it is that Omar could repeat the behavior of his oppressors and become one of them. He could connect with adults that care and become an "expert witness" - one who has been through the suffering and come out on the other side to become a voice for healing.

The birthplace of revenge is in abuse and violence. Omar knows both. Yet, Omar also has seen the resiliency of a mother and of intercessors found in the AID agencies that could facilitate a different path - a path of healing and advocacy that says this will happen to no more children.

When Michael asked me to help, Omar's story became my story. It is now your story. Please pray for the Omars of this famine and for those of you that can do more - volunteer and donate so we can place counselors on the ground to bring healing to the soul, the mind, and the body. We can do this; therefore, we must do this!

The story of Claudia and Omar require similar responses. Separated by time and distance, both children are victims of choices made by adults. For Claudia the skills she champions are the result of teachers who care and for Omar, the pain he has experienced will shape and define his future unless adults make resources available to assist in his healing and restoration.

The numbers are sometimes numbing. There are 2.2 billion children in the world and 1 billion of them live in poverty. In the United States, 17 million children wake up daily without the promise of a hot meal and globally 13,000 children die every day because of hunger. Staggering numbers! However, they seem to fade into the landscape of our competing interests and concerns. As a nation, as a community of faith, we cannot let the incredible need overwhelm us. Each number serves as an alarm that our indifference or refusal to make desperate connections has consumed another portion of our future and our potential.

Chapter Six - Horizons of Hope

Jurgen Moltmann in a surprisingly brief, but power, book entitled *In the End – The Beginning: The Life of Hope*, writes: *So God comes to meet men and women out of his future, and in their history reveals to them new, open horizons, which entice them to set forth into the unknown and invite them to the beginning of the new.*[3] There are so many themes in this telling statement. The fact that God meets men and women places less emphasis on our vain attempts to please or satisfy God with our puny works or struggles. He breaks into our lives and He comes to us out of His future. God comes to us out of the future and exposes our history and provides new meaning, new horizons to scan that give new and powerful definitions to our lives.

Voices from the Night relates the history of some of our children. For the most part, I witnessed the stories. I observed their struggle to speak, to survive, and to ultimately triumph. I have not been able, because of time and distance, to track their journeys, but each day brings an echo from their experience.

A war still rages in Afghanistan and the peace process in the Middle East is in shambles, yet, I am reminded of children I saw nearly ten years ago in a

[3] Jurgen Moltmann, In the End – The Beginning: The Life of Hope, (Minneapolis: The Fortress Press), 2004. p.87

refugee camp in Gaza. The faint echo lost over time is returning as a shout in my ears and conscience, for as I visited these children they ran to me and my truck with hope and acceptance. There was no malice or anger, no anti-American sentiment. You could see in their eyes youthful confidence unclouded by poverty, hunger, or powerlessness. In this particular encounter, there were about 30 children running, skipping, jumping, and offering greetings. They were not begging; there were no expectations – all they wanted was contact. The promise of a greeting embraced in peace and warmth instead of the sound of rolling tanks or the crackling of guns that would often send them running for cover.

In these environments, I am struck by the resiliency of youth born out of the pain or grief of life. Their resilience demands presence. They seem to cry out in their strife, their laughter, and their exuberance a demand for attention. *You will hear me and you will know that I exist and offer something to this engagement known as life.* "The cards may spell defeat, the opportunities seem limited in comparison, and on any given day the rest of the world does not give a damn that I exist or have the right to exist. Yet, my life is about horizons. I have so little to look back on and so much to look forward to. First steps are never backwards, they are always forward."

Children portray images of vulnerability and resiliency. I was impressed and saddened by the many pictures that came out of the island communities of the Indian Ocean following the December 26, 2004 earthquake and subsequent tsunami. This natural catastrophe killed over 150,000, left 5 million individual homeless, and cost an already war-torn region billions of dollars in property losses and human suffering. Their innocence was swept away by a force of nature so great that it flattened concrete, swept whole buildings off their pedestals, and floated heavy vehicles like so many bathtub toys. Children, by estimates, constituted over a third of the human loss. As days passed, we heard stories of the resiliency of youth in the face of so much loss. Again, the voices come from the horizon of hope.

The conflicting images of parents grieving and of parents finding their children tore at the soul. It was both a season for grieving and a season for rejoicing. The magnitude of the loss and the long-term impact on families and communities will be difficult to compute. It puts into relief the chasm between the rich nations of the northern hemisphere and the poor nations of the south. The initial response of the United States was a paltry $15 million in relief. International criticism and our lack of awareness about the full measure of the devastation have now compelled us to respond with $350 million in financial commitments. More was to come and the international community responded with significant resources. The catastrophe, has by its own force, silenced the warring parties engulfed in a civil war. To be sure, this is a temporary respite in a climate already ripe for struggle.

How the "Christian" West responds to this predominately Muslim world will no doubt set the stage for generations of cooperation or conflict. Ultimately, the choice will be ours. These young voices watching and experiencing our response will cry out in praise or they will deride our actions in the courts of public opinion. If the West fails to navigate this terrain fraught with both opportunity and peril, we will have participated in our own long and agonizing destruction. The unknown will be a world of darkness and despair.

I cannot help but compare these choices with those I experience as a new grandfather. In the nine months following the tsunami, we went from 0 to 4 grandchildren - three boys and one beautiful girl. I approached grandfather-hood with considerable apprehension and detachment. Between my wife and me (blended family), we have eight children. I have maintained, between college, church missions, cars, etc., we had more than done our duty and fulfilled our responsibility. The grandkids could come by and sail on grandpa's boat, they could play with his John Deere toy tractor collection, they could read his books, and occasionally, if I am in town – spend the night. But don't talk to me about their general welfare, their housing, their education, or any of the hundreds of other details that will make up their young and impressionable lives. That is now the responsibility of their parents. I did my tour – they can do theirs.

All was well and good, until I held the first little cuddly boy in my arms. All four of these children have me wrapped around their little fingers. As of this writing, we have eighteen grandkids. So, I am searching for more string and more arms. I love the times when we can all be together.

I have cancelled sailing trips, spent way too much money, and altered my basic lifestyle to accommodate their schedules. I can't wait until I see them the next time. My lovely wife is enjoying this transformation in my personality.

As I examine their growth and watch their changing features over the weeks since their births, I am amazed at what I see. They respond to sounds, to light, to smiles, to warm embraces. They scream with indignation as their bare bottoms are lifted to the cold air to receive another diaper. I watch tears fall down their soft cheeks and wonder how many more will follow in the course of their lives. I see their smiles and dimples emerging and speculate on the charms they will utilize to flirt and to convince their partners of just how clever they are. Most of all, I am curious about the grey matter between their ears. Just what will they do with their minds and their hearts? What will capture their passion – what will seize their enthusiasm and take them to places they never cared for? They are our children of hope and they pull us into horizons never before explored. They call for me and beg me to follow them into their lives to see things I can only imagine. Occasionally on their journey, they will pause and look behind to their ancestors to gain some assurance that this course, this path, this direction is truly worthy of pursuit. They will be met with smiles of encouragement and a simple shrug of the shoulders that suggests – who knows where these roads will lead. However, what would life be if we did not take this course? What things would be left undiscovered? What thoughts would not have been explored? What dreams would be unfulfilled if we failed to search the horizon for new dreams and new realities? Ah, I have confidence in the children I have seen and met – they will indeed find these horizons.

Finding and Living in the Unknown

Strange is the world of the unknown! To the unknown we offer a variety of responses. We can choose to remain ignorant and simply leave it alone – after all, we can't know what we don't know. We can flee it and consume ourselves in activities that prevent us from seeing the unknown. You know the type – too busy to see, to feel, to think, to hear, or to act. Or, as with all great explorers, we can embrace the unknown and plunge into its depths waiting for the thrill of discovery. The focus of our search becomes how discovery may transform our lives by giving us new insights, new visions, and new challenges. Somehow this last approach contributes to our own rescue – our own salvation. Those of us who have worked in the field of international development, substance abuse, crime, and violence prevention have seen the stagnant minds of indifferent communities or the calloused bureaucrats that fail to grasp that we are engaged in a human enterprise that demands flexibility and timely responses. We struggle on – looking for those new horizons. What do those horizons hold for us?

When I came to this work nearly 20 years ago, I did not anticipate the pandemic of AIDS in Africa or the horror and costs of methamphetamine abuse among rural Americans or in tribal communities, nor did I see the destruction caused by youth gun violence and alcohol abuse. Currently we are seeing reports in the City of Chicago where nearly 30 people a month are gunned down by senseless violence. The conflict between Khartoum and the newly organized government in the South Sudan is creating a refugee situation that takes thousands of lives monthly. The world stands by while women are sexually assaulted and children abandoned while parents and older children search for food. The challenges in the developing world often seem insurmountable. There is an endless amount of pain and suffering caused by corruption, severe poverty, and hopelessness caused by gender bias.

Politics in the developing world, particularly in Africa, is undergoing significant change. Emerging from the generation of political leaders that gave birth to the independence movements, the new leadership faces a choice. Will they revert to autocratic regimes that promote the "strong man" approach to politics or will they embrace the empowerment models that give power to people and foster economic growth and development? The answer to that question remains in the future. This part of the unknown has enormous consequences for nearly a billion people.

Currently, the Horn of Africa and Kenya are experiencing the worst drought in 40 years and famine is overtaking the region. Approximately 3,000 children are dying each month. After three tours of the Dadaab Refugee Camp near the Somali border, one is struck by the magnitude of this crisis and the resiliency of its survivors. Further, in famine relief stations throughout Kenya and the Horn, you can see the strength and character of individuals responding to the current crisis.

I have been working with Nazarene Compassionate Ministries since August of 2011, to help facilitate famine relief planning and activities in the Horn of Africa and Kenya. Early in the process, I started keeping a journal to record eyewitness accounts and stories about the courage and strength of the people we met in Ethiopia, Kenya, South Sudan, and Somalia. This journal will forever be my record of the horrors of extreme poverty and the hope of a faithful intervention.

Journal Entry - June 15, 2012 - I just returned from Lodwar, Kenya, a dry and desolate part of northwestern Kenya near Lake Turkana. It is a forsaken place where nearly 850,000 people roam through the deforested pasturelands that are now dotted with an occasional acacia tree and scrub brush. The dust is forever blowing and the heat is impossible to escape. Here 700 homesteads or approximately 2,800 primary beneficiaries receive emergency food relief from the Church of the Nazarene in what is the worst drought in nearly 40 years. The $100,000 donated by the Church for Lodwar is the story of the power of the particular and the promise of a structural solution to their predicament.

The Particular: The Lodwar Church of the Nazarene has a team of organized, disciplined, and compassionate volunteers who wait for the truck with its precious load of beans, maize, and cooking oil. The 500 beneficiaries wait patiently while the team organizes the precious commodities soon to be delivered into the hands of a starving population. In the Lake Turkana region, where starvation and famine are a way of life, waiting for food distribution can be dangerous and precarious. The Church hired security and after the truck was unloaded, we began the very organized process of distributing the grain. Each homestead received two buckets of maize and one bucket of beans. Each were then given a liter of cooking oil. I thought of conducting individual interviews, but it was simply too overwhelming. The stories would vary by nuance but the substance would be pretty much the same. These are people that have been largely ignored by the politicians and the global community. They are starving despite the presence of dozens of government organizations and NGOs (secular and religious). They are thankful that the Nazarenes have delivered on their promise - six months of food supply while they develop a sustainable agriculture plan.

Standing patiently in line are hundreds of women dressed in their traditional Turkana costumes with beads coiled around their necks. Children pick through the dirt separating spilled maize from the sandy soil. They had in their possession small clear plastic bags to hold and protect their findings.

One of the more startling if not fascinating scenes I observed, was that of a young child of five or six who showed up on his own carrying two very tiny black trash bags to claim possession of his allotment. He was not registered, but he noticed people had two bags - one for maize - one for beans. So he brought his two bags and assumed, that because he was smaller, he should have small bags. He boldly walked through the registration line bypassing the bureaucracy that required him to produce an ID, receive a number, and be thumb printed. He wound his way past the security and found himself standing behind a lady already thumb printed and ready to receiver her maize. When it was his turn, he opened his one bag and the volunteer was startled by his presence. There was no way two full buckets of maize were going to fit into that small black trash bag. She asked for his number. He just stared. The volunteer informed him that he did not qualify. But he protested asserting he had his two bags and therefore he qualified. The volunteer was extremely disciplined and was skeptical. Children are often used to do the bidding of adults that may or may not qualify for a project. However, in consultation with the pastor, I pointed out, it was unlikely that he was there on behalf of an adult or he would have had in his possession two larger bags. The pastor smiled and said "Good point." "He is probably a street kid and an orphan" the pastor further clarified. He nodded to the volunteer and said, "Fill his bags." I stood beside him as his eyes lit up with satisfaction. Now he had two bags filled with maize and grain. He passed up the cooking oil. The look on his face was more about status than the need for food. Like everybody else, he had his own food supply.

Structural Solution: One child fed - but the pastor has a vision for a more sustainable approach. Rev. Sam and Rev. Oketch, the NCO Coordinator for Kenya are working to create a compassionate infrastructure to foster sustainable agriculture. The 700 beneficiaries of the emergency food relief program have raised 150,000 Kenyan Shillings ($1,760) toward a goal of 550,000 ksh ($6,470) to purchase 50 acres of land. From the famine relief funds and a gift from a generous Nazarene family, a water system will be put in place to support the development of plots of land for the 500 participants. Soon food will be growing and these 500 homesteads will begin the process of moving from aid to development. I challenged the pastor and beneficiaries to raise another 100,000 ksh ($1,176) and to achieve a 250,000 ksh goal and our foundation, the Servant Forge Foundation will match the rest. This is a partnership in development with a people who have given the widow's mite to purchase the land.

There is hope in Lodwar and Turkana because 700 homesteads want to move from dependency to food independence. The 50 acres will give them the needed food security they must have in order to survive. The Global Church stood in the gap - the local Church planned a long-term solution, and the partners on the ground with Nazarene Compassionate Ministries will assure success.

When I see these experiences in my work and journey, I often find myself reflecting on what this one little intervention with the child may have contributed. Where will he be ten years from now or twenty years from now? However, with the acquisition of 50 acres of land, access to water, and a determined community - I also can see small farms, children playing and going to school instead of searching for food and water. This is a good project and sustainable. This is why the Church must always find a way to stand in the gap.

While hope for this young boy is pretty thin. He is in survival mode and any chance of education or secure housing is remote. Yet, once again, I witnessed a resiliency that transcended age, culture, and geography. They were resourceful, creative, and determined. Their response was to look at the current reality, figure out how to navigate through it or find an alternative.

I have witnessed that response on many occasions. In 2010, our firm facilitated a summit on youth employment in Kenya. Sixty percent of the youth population between the ages of 18-35 are unemployed and have little prospect for meaningful work. This reality has created the right kind of tinder to ignite a fire that leads to violence and mass hysteria. The summit was designed to identify solutions to both job readiness and job creation. Following the summit, a young man from the slums of Korogocho in Nairobi approached me with a question regarding the relationship between substance abuse and youth unemployment. Given the trajectory of my career, I was intrigued by his question. I agreed to meet with him following the summit.

Brian Odour is a quiet and unassuming young man with a personal history that is anything but normal. His father and brother died of AIDS and his mother is currently living with AIDS. The Catholic Church in Korogocho found Brian and they saw a talent and mind that deserved every opportunity to succeed. They covered his school expenses and he finally made it to the University of Nairobi where is currently preparing for a career in medicine. Brian is voice of hope and determination.

Brian refuses to be silenced. I facilitate numerous meetings in Nairobi, mostly focused on youth employment, substance abuse, gender-based violence, poverty eradication, and governance reform. When and where possible - Brian is there. He shows up with this infectious smile that turns a dark room into one of laughter and empathy. He is bold with his questions and he is always challenging the way his friends and colleagues think. He is not content with the status quo, but he is not a crusader. He gets things done as a young man with a voice, however soft and articulate, that commands respect and creates a following.

I have often challenged my colleagues to never give up on a child. I have seen horrific conditions and deplorable behavior in gang-filled communities, murder, rape, and mutilation. Yet, in interviewing thousands of young people across my journey - as angry as I might get, as depressing as it may seem, there is always something in youth that captures my attention. It is a spark anchored in their belief that they will be here tomorrow. Ours is to come along side them, hear their voice, and when possible join them or include them in the chorus of voices fighting for change or their place at the community table. The voice from the night will either sing hope or shout us down in anger as we attempt to silence it.

Bring me the Horizon

In the closing scene of *The Pirates of the Caribbean: The Curse of the Black Pearl*, Captain Jack Sparrow, played by Johnny Depp, has once again been rescued by his faithful crew. He stands squarely behind the wheel of his vessel, and with that ever so charming smile, he orders - "Bring me the horizon." I love those words. It captures my own sense of adventure and my own vision of where God would have me live and work. I am all about horizon thinking and horizon projects. I have also discovered that through horizon projects children and youth pull us into their future.

I just got off a Skype call with my eight-year-old grandson Brendan - a budding hockey player. Over the past year as he sought to master the goalie position on the ice, I discovered he does not like to talk about the games he has lost (most of them), but he prefers talking about the next tournament or the next match or what he must do to stop the pucks that come firing in his direction. He is all about tomorrow and is truly a horizon thinker.

Impatient youth want a voice. They want to lead. They want to be heard now. They see many of us as obstructionists to their plans and their future. As adults, we must stop looking over the waters we have already sailed. Rather, we need to find waters on the horizon and come alongside the youth of our world as they search for their safe ports and distant and unexplored lands.

Moltmann said it well, *So God comes to meet men and women out of his future, and in their history reveals to them new, open horizons, which entice them to set forth into the unknown and invite them to the beginning of the new*. I think that says it all. The voices from the night are the voices that shape and define the "new." These are voices filled with hope and imagination and they are voices that over time give way to new and different ones. The dynamic nature of God's presence is never stagnant nor merely a holding on to the past - but rather a wind that blows us into the excitement of the unknown and pushes us into unchartered waters of a future filled with hope and promise.

Chapter Seven - I Witnessed

The roads in eastern Ethiopia are difficult to navigate. They are water filled "canyons" with few markers to indicate direction. Large supply trucks, weighted down by their precious cargoes, are up to their axles in mud. Six of us were traveling in a Land Cruiser - an indispensable piece of equipment for this part of the world. One wag commented, "You want to get to Masai Mara, drive a Land Rover, you want to get home, drive a Land Cruiser."

This five-hour one-way trip to several communities seemed like just one more humanitarian mission. For reasons I cannot totally explain, it became so much more. Godare, a border community in dispute between Ethiopia and Somalia, hosts refugees while raided by rebels and terrorists alike. It is five miles from the Somali border. In just three months the camp has grown from 2,000 people to 25,000 people. Yet, international aid organizations such as UN agencies are not there. The border dispute prevents these agencies from doing their important work.

The four days we spent in eastern Ethiopia have affected me in a ways that no other journey has. In fact, I have not been able to write about it because anything I say seems premature, self-righteous, or judgmental. The misery of famine and starvation, complicated by conflicts between faiths and political powers, washed over me and seemed to silence me. I felt broken on a rock of hopelessness that spilled any self-preserving detachment on to the ground to be soaked up by the horror of the moment. While nature caused the famine, politics and religion exacerbated it. This suffering is preventable.

For four days, I witnessed the choices made by parents and caregivers to either neglect or abandon their children because of starvation and fear. I watched human migration across barren lands in search of food, water, or safety. But perhaps, most disconcerting, I was a witness to the world's neglect. For certain, the usual suspects were present in Eastern Ethiopia - from faith-based NGOs seeking to put a finger in the dike to avert human suffering to a few global educators operating a school. There was no outrage, no anger, no urgency or call to action. People, both benefactors and beneficiaries moved through the motions of survival. There was a terrible sense of "normal." I had seen this all before, but this time it just seemed different. It felt like I was becoming a witness to the worst in human experience.

A few days later, I came home to the hysterical debates of Congress and political campaigns during which the famine in the Horn of Africa and Kenya never received a remark. In fact, in all the year-end reflections of 2011, nobody mentioned the famine and the number of people dying. As a witness to this horrible situation, I felt isolated and alone and every time I attempted to describe what I felt, people would simply stare. I felt like I was being a killjoy to the holiday festivities. Despite pleas by the ONE Foundation and other relief organizations with media capacity, nobody paid attention to the realities that over 30,000 children have died in the past three months. I went through my normal Christmas rituals of children and grandchildren, but I also felt lost and adrift.

I have grown stronger in recent days because of another fact associated with this experience - I was not only a witness to incredible suffering, I was also a witness to amazing courage. A group of Christians reached out to Muslims and offered them food and water. Because of religious conflict and persecution, I cannot mention their names nor their communities - but I can try to describe their acts. In this case, a small but committed Christian community worshipping underground had access to food and grains which they freely distributed to their Muslim neighbors. These Muslim neighbors told me how greatly they appreciated this act of compassion and care and how they wanted to join hands with their new friends to confront the immediate crisis of hunger and conflict. I witnessed Muslims embracing Christians and expressing gratitude for something so basic as a cup of water. I realized at that moment; I was witnessing the power of community action. Action at the community level that makes a neighbor more than an abstract concept but a person with a face, a person with a family, a person with dreams. These actions transcend religious and political conflict.

What has not been achieved in conference rooms, parliaments, or in complex negotiations is being achieved by tender acts of mercy. These acts are made possible by committed and dedicated individuals, often supported by generous donors thousands of miles away. Suddenly, I felt the bridge. Many people in the US and other parts of the developed world provide resources; courageous individuals living in remote parts of the Horn of Africa take those resources and convert them into sustainable acts of love and grace. Geopolitics aside in the global conflict between Muslim and Christian - faith based organizations and individuals go into the darkness of human suffering. They confront the noise of hate and subdue the violence with acts of charity and compassion. Alas, I have been a witness to the worst of humanity and the best of humanity transformed by grace.

Another tension in the world of complacency that defines our political and social discourse is the issue of women. Women virtually disappearing, being denied access to food and water, and worst of all being treated with sexual abuse and starvation.

Our Mothers and our Sisters – We Must Share Their Voice

The number 107 million launched off the pages of the *Sunday New York Times Magazine* like a missile exploding across my conscience. Is it possible that there are currently 107 million women who have gone missing because of rape, torture, infanticide, starvation and neglect? In the 21st Century, modernity has permitted the enslavement and abuse of women at a rate that numbs the imagination. One hundred thirty million women around the world have been subjected to genital cutting. In Ghana, 21% of young women surveyed reported that their sexual initiation was by rape. [i] In the midst of the genocides that have occurred since the holocaust – Cambodia, Rwanda, East Timor and most recently, Darfur the trafficking and slaughter of women overshadows the numbers found in these political nightmares. Even in the genocides of the past 50 years – one wonders how many of the victims were women or victims because they were women?

Eleven trips to sub-Saharan Africa in the past two years have brought these numbers into sharp relief. Focusing on HIV/AIDS and the pandemic that is killing 3,000 children a day on the continent of Africa one sees the devastation this disease has had on the women of these cultures. When men acquire the "sickness" the women nurse them to health or stay at their side until the disease is abated or consumes the men. When women acquire "dirty blood" the men leave and abandon them in pursuit of other women less dirty. Women living with HIV/AIDS are found living by themselves or in small support communities of other women living with the disease. Their survival is dependent upon a network of care supporters that roam the countryside of sub-Saharan Africa providing access to precious ARVs or nutrition.

In the midst of this reality stands the Church. The Church, quite often is the only thing that prevents these survivors from falling off the face of the earth. However, one is forced to ask, to what extent has faith, the Church, the Mosque, the Synagogue or the traditional faith healer in villages across Africa contributed to this neglect and to the marginalization of women in all cultures? I continue to be outraged by a superficial theology that justifies an inferior status for women. Every church, every faith that "proof texts" its way across its scriptures justifying the exclusion of women or relegating them to the back pew of leadership should be called to repentance. Like the prophet Amos, we should stand outside the city gates of religion and cry *Woe to You* for the sin that is gender discrimination. We must no longer tolerate governments and leaders that abuse and neglect our mothers and our sisters. These behaviors in policy, in practice and in belief are an abomination to God. The gender silos that once separated us were shattered in the biblical admonition – there is neither male nor female.

We must approach the institutions of our faith(s) and confront them and condemn them if necessary when they say no to a woman simply because of her gender. Faiths that exclude women and tolerate their abuse or submit them to torturous rituals and deny them voice in schools or pulpits should fall to their knees in repentance. As harsh as it may sound, these very acts are in solidarity with those that practice infanticide of young female babies, rape and torture of teenage girls and deny young women access to education. These gender biases permit the powerful to justify exclusion and when you can justify exclusion you are complicit in the marginalization and victimization of women.

In recent months the Obama administration, through former Secretary of State Hillary Rodham Clinton has catapulted this issue before the global community. Gender and women's health issues are part of the Millennium Development Goals (MDGs) and in a new book published by Nicholas D. Kristof and his colleague and spouse, Sheryl WuDunn; they argue that women's rights should be the "cause of our time." I am perplexed that these movements are initiated by government and media. Where is the voice of the faith community? These women are our mothers and our sisters, they are our wives and our friends – the Church cannot remain silent but must set the example by removing any and all barriers to women's access to all roles and responsibilities in the institutions of faith.

Any religious leader who advocates for gender exclusion in the full work of their faith is by definition a false prophet. Any religious tradition who dares to proclaim the Kingdom of God and discriminates against the full participation of women is by its action and definition a bearer of a false truth. The voices of 107 million women have been silenced. Their screams for help are the screams of our own mothers and sisters – we must all share in their voice and that voice must rise to a shout that will tumble the walls of exclusion that deny them safety, security, health, education and the joys of full participation in our global community.

Gender inequality remains an issue that continues to frustrate development and justice globally. Whether you are sitting on the sidelines of American politics listening to the debate over women's issues or living in a village in northern Kenya, women continue to be exasperated by the glass ceiling that prevents them from achieving their goals and realizing their dreams.

There are extremes in these discussions that should cause our blood to boil. A 70-year-old woman in northern Kenya is forced to stay in her homestead because she is widowed and refuses to have intercourse with her husband's brother in order to restore her to the full community. She is property. To be sure, for those of us who claim the Hebrew or Christian scriptures as our authority, the woman as property issue continues to justify our relegation of women to second class citizenry. Or, in the United States, a woman's access to the corporate board room or full service in the military is a cause for concern, because she has a menstrual cycle.

I am frustrated by the efforts of good people in my religious tradition that believe women should not lead, manage, or speak because culturally determined remarks by the Apostle Paul. Yet, when you look and actually count, as I have, 60% of the personal encounters Jesus has in the New Testament involve women. Jesus was the first religious leader to suggest, no, not only suggest, but affirm, that women could have salvation. What a thought! Further, even the Apostle Paul affirmed in his epistle to the Galatians, "There is neither Jew nor Greek, slave nor free, male nor female, for you are all one in Christ Jesus." (Galatians 3:28). Religious leaders, who express, in their not so subtle tokenism, "Don't worry, your day will come" play into a culture of bias that damages both the mission and work of the Church. Maybe bias is too soft of a word - how is this not an artifact of gender bigotry? Even the word sexist softens the position.

I heard one wag recently remark, men should treat women as we would want men to treat our daughters. This is probably a good start for moving beyond our prejudices. I have two daughters and three stepdaughters. I tell you right now - any man get in the way of their goals or their right to equal access, and they will have me to fight.

We can stop this with a quick assessment: 1) How do we treat the women in our lives and do we treat them as children of God? 2) Are we prepared to speak up when men demean women and describe them as only sex objects? 3) Can we or will we advocate for women in the placement of key leadership and management positions within our organizations? 4) Are we prepared to work within an environment that promotes an equal playing field that allows women the same access afforded to men?

If you cannot positively affirm these actions, then we have some distance to go before we can affirm that Paul was right, "neither male nor female." Salvation is the great affirmation. Jesus had no problem asserting that women had access to salvation; therefore, they should access to jobs, leadership, and serve equally with the men of the world.

We will never change cultural norms around bias or prejudice until we change them in the faith communities that shape our values. All the monotheistic religions have a horrible history when it comes to women. This is why in the 21st century these religions have become increasingly irrelevant. I am amazed in my own religions tradition (Christian, Protestant, Wesleyan, Nazarene) at the lip service given to women's access but the failure to include women in key leadership positions. My tradition is hardly alone on this issue.

Robin Meyers in his work, *The Underground Church: Reclaiming the Subversive Way of Jesus* made the following observation: "How ironic then, that according to our story, women were last at the cross and first at the tomb - yet in some churches they are still not allowed to preach or hold positions of authority. Without women there would be no church. This is not a liberal or conservative position, but rather an historical reality." (159).

I used to stress with my students in Church History that in the early Christian community, the Church before Irenaeus (c. 130 - c.200) and Constantine (d. 337), women held key leadership positions and were responsible for the most important ministry of the church, hospitality - the care and feeding of the "stranger." Hospitality in the contemporary church has been reduced to an industry and church suppers. In early Christianity, hospitality was central to the moral foundation of the church. Hospitality equaled Christian morality. If we recaptured the meaning of hospitality, it would transform the way we relate to all kinds of different and diverse populations.

Over the centuries, layers of bureaucratic and dogmatic protectionism by men have kept women at a distance - and have excluded them from leadership. Jesus would not recognize his community in the modern church. Nor, interestingly enough, despite our proof-texting of certain passages from the Apostle Paul, would Paul recognize the community. We have totally underestimated the power of Paul's statement to the Galatians and its ramifications for the life of the early Christian community.

Again, things we can do today:

1. Assess how your church includes women in leadership positions and encourage inclusion.
2. Don't be afraid of thinking in "quotas." Nobody wants to be a token, but nobody wants to be excluded. In race relations in the United States - quota programs have worked. They guaranteed access and contributed to

greater participation by minorities in all facets of life.

3. Encourage women to enter the ministry and set up awareness programs with congregations about the historical involvement and important role women play in leadership.

4. Don't talk about equal rights outside the church unless you are prepared to practice it inside the church. Leaders will champion the involvement of women in all aspects of the life of the church.

5. Facilitate gender awareness when it comes to abuse, neglect, child protection, and engagement in the broader community. Women are disproportionately victimized by crime, violence, and sexual abuse. The church and its leadership should be a safe place for women to gather and learn.

6. Train and equip church boards on how to recruit, nurture, and learn from women in ministry. Be intentional.

There are many other things you can and should do. Many of you are already doing them. It is time we put action behind our words. We hurt ourselves by excluding the majority of members in our congregations and communities - women.

The Voice of Malala

Sitting by the bay in San Diego overlooking the cityscape and centering down for a few quiet moments, I could not escape the news of the morning. On Tuesday, in Pakistan, the Taliban attempted to assassinate Malala Yousafzai, the 14-year-old activist who advocates for the right of young girls to be educated. Pakistan continues to fail to secure and protect the rights of women. The Taliban, in defiance of their own scriptures and threatened by the voice of a teenager, ignored the teachings of the Prophet Mohammed, "The one who is not kind to children, is not amongst us."

I cannot escape this story! I am a witness to this historical event and as a witness, I am now complicit. It raises a number of questions that should challenge the global community. While it is about the individual shooting of a young adolescent, it is also about the environment that necessitates the voice of a 14-year-old to speak out about injustices within education. Nobody else would speak - so she had to. To be sure, her voice reached the global advocacy community and she was recognized and awarded with several international prizes.

Malala began this journey when she was only 11. She cast a light on a system of injustices that denied girls the right to be informed and to contribute. For this, she was celebrated globally, but nearly killed in her own country. This is a voice from the night that insisted that her country would be better if women were educated.

The WHY questions jump out at us.
- Why would a young girl need to advocate for her right to be educated?
- Why are men of this country or any country threatened by women being educated?
- Where were the adult advocates that should be speaking out and allowing the Malalas of the world to be focused on their education and well, quite simply, being a teenager?
- If this were one of my daughters - what would I do?

Global poverty contributes to conditions that threaten or undermine individual rights. In the social Darwinist world we live in, resources are secured by the strong. When individuals are denied those human rights then the conditions of poverty only worsen. We are cutting out a talent and resource pool that could make us all stronger. The Taliban is a weak and cowardly organization whose hate trumps their political agenda and leaves them with no recourse but to silence a child. We must not allow this violence to showcase the worst in all of us - a tendency to remain silent against such violence and oppression.

I left my quiet time on the bay that morning thinking of Matthew 18:5-6, "Whoever receives one such child in my name receives me, but whoever causes one of these little ones who believe in me to sin, it would be better for him to have a great millstone fastened around his neck and to be drowned in the depth of the sea." (RSV) I confess, I pray for my Muslim sister, Malala, this morning that she recovers and continues to be a voice. I pray for all of us to see her as our family in the quest for gender equality and access. I also admit to praying that the Taliban responsible for this cowardly act would meet a few millstones.

Our pursuit for justice must always include compassion and compassion will create the opportunity for us to tell our story. As I Peter 3:15-16 point out, "But in your hearts set apart Christ as Lord. Always be prepared to give an answer to everyone who asks you to give the reason for the hope that you have. But do this with gentleness and respect, keeping a clear conscience, so that those who speak maliciously against your good behavior in Christ may be ashamed of their slander."

Be prepared to give an answer. I witnessed firsthand a woman whose life had been transformed by the acts of compassion and justice. These acts led to inclusion in the Kingdom and the Church.

Inok Elimlim Akaale, a 63-year-old traditional Turkana woman is a new member of the Church of the Nazarene, the congregation we partner with on famine relief. Akaale has lived a pastoral life herding goats and cattle in the rough and barren lands surrounding Lake Turkana - Kenya's largest lake. She has moved every two or three years in search of needed grassland and water. She, along with 850,000 people that populate Turkana County on the border of South Sudan, has known famine most of her life.

The Church of the Nazarene in Lodwar, with funds provided by the global church, purchased emergency food for over 700 preselected beneficiaries. I had the privilege of interviewing Akaale and asking her why she attended this local church. Her answers illustrate the intersection between compassion and evangelism.

> Jim: Why do you come to this Church?
>
> Akaale: I come for three reasons.
>
> Jim: Three reasons (said with a smile) - What are those three reasons?
>
> Akaale: I have been coming here since the month of May and I came here first because of the food distribution the Nazarenes were providing. I just keep coming. I was here when you brought the white people (Wazungu) - a short Muzungu woman hugged me and told me Jesus cared about me. (She held her hand to the ground to emphasize "short.")

Jim: What did that mean to you?

Akaale: I saw Jesus in her. (She started crying.)

Jim: What are the other two reasons?

Akaale: I come here because Jesus does not hit me.

Jim: People hit you?

Akaale: My father did and my husband did. (Both died of AIDS)

Jim: But here Jesus will not hit you?

Akaale: No, and also Jesus feeds me.

Jim: Why do you say Jesus instead of Church? (Translator had to sort that question out.)

Akaale: The Church is Jesus and Jesus always says welcome with an open hand and not a raised fist. (She raised her hand in a fist motion and pretended to swing at me. We laughed).

The Famine Relief Initiative of the Church included emergency food, sustainable agriculture, and counseling services for women victimized by violence. Akaale knew famine, abuse, and neglect. She is a survivor and a survivor who found Jesus through the compassion of a church.

We are all witnesses to the hurt, the suffering, and yes, the joy that comes from coming along side our friends and neighbors. As a witness, I now have a responsibility and a moral obligation to engage. The writer of I John underscores this truth when he wrote: "This is love: not that we loved God, but that he loved us and sent his Son as an atoning sacrifice for our sins. Dear friends, since God so loved us, we also ought to love one another." (I John 4:10-11). The word "ought" in this passage comes from the Greek word *automate;* where we derive our word automatic. The failure to respond "automatically" may indicate our failure to grasp the depth and power of God's love for us. His grace is the impulse for service.

Chapter Eight - The Empathy Bridge - When Their Voice Becomes Your Voice

I shared previously that the most dangerous prayer we can pray is the one that asks God to help us see as He sees, to hear as He hears, and to feel as He feels. When you dare to pray that prayer, all things change and you are never the same when facing a challenge, a relationship or an experience. This prayer puts you into the middle of the storm - it calls for an empathic response or experience. Empathy is what makes it possible for us to hear the voices from the night. Empathy puts you into the experience of the other - it puts you into their life, their understanding, their world unprotected by culture, distance or time. Suddenly two voices become one and while differentiated by age, by culture, by gender, by language, it expresses itself in a unified message that resonates in the mind of the observer.

Sympathy is something you feel *for* someone or something - empathy is something you feel *with* someone. Sympathy is an expression that keeps you outside the world of the subject. It may be driven by an event or crisis, but sympathy for someone allows you a measure of distance. Sympathy does not allow you to participate in the pain or the reality of the person whose life is in crisis. Empathy, on the other hand takes you into the experience and allows you to feel, to taste, to touch the experience of the other.

Empathy as a psycho-social experience was first articulated or defined in the late 19th century and came out of the emerging field of psychiatry. Empathy as a concept was an attempt to translate the experience or relationship between the therapist and the patient. The field of psychiatry remains complicated, but in its inception, pioneers in the field tried to understand the role of the therapist and their relationship to the patient's disorders. Empathy was the bridge between patient and therapist.

Therapy is an intimate experience that requires language, emotion, and a depth of engagement that can create risk for the participants. We enter the therapeutic relationship particularly the efficacious relationship voluntarily. We anticipate a positive or healing outcome. There is a degree of vulnerability that in and of itself can be transformative.

I am certain that my work in development, substance abuse prevention and treatment, and poverty elimination is anchored in an empathic heart forged in a relationship with Jesus Christ. My first experiences as a child witnessing an injustice, whether it was the way people treated "blacks" in the South or the difference between those who were affluent and those of us who were not, shaped who I am and fired the emotions that demanded some kind of reaction. To this day, I can remember one such an experience that forever changed my heart and my attitude toward race.

It was 1958 and I was eight- years old. The United States was still a nation divided against itself. The racial divide found its expression in Jim Crow laws. In the South, you could still see signs of *Whites Only* or separate water fountains for Negroes and Whites. It was in this environment that I found myself in Tupelo, Mississippi with my parents and older brother.

We were on our way to Florida from Kansas City for a family vacation. A few miles outside of Tupelo on a two-lane asphalt road, our brown 1958 Oldsmobile blew a tire. In the process, a lug bolt broke making it difficult to mount the spare tire. After assessing the situation, my father, a skilled mechanic, decided to remove the wheel plate that held the tire to the axle. He and I would walk to Tupelo to find a garage. It was July and I could feel the heat from the road on my feet through the thin soles of my Converse tennis shoes. It was one of those hot, humid days that allowed no escape.

We walked past cotton fields where we could see the black faces of sharecroppers against the white blossoms of cotton as they bent over plants pulling their harvest from thorny bowls of dry shells. Dad explained the process.

On the horizon, we could see the familiar sign of a Sinclair station. As we approached, we could see it was not only a filling station but also a garage with a small market. As we walked through the doors, about 20 sharecroppers stood between the counter and us. We hesitated and suddenly I could feel the firm grip of my father's hand around my hand. The gesture created more fear than security. Why was he holding my hand, I thought. Suddenly from the counter someone shouted, "White man." A path opened and we walked to the counter.

In the midst of this sea of black faces, I felt conspicuous - I felt exposed for being white. I also felt very thirsty. My dad caught me staring at a pop machine in the corner of the room. He handed me a quarter and nodded as if to say, "Go ahead get a drink." I walked confidently through the crowd and put my quarter in the black coin box. I lifted the lid and felt the blast of cold refrigerated air hit my face. Before me were choices of soda hanging like soldiers in single file on tracks with an opening at each end. After a few seconds, I grabbed an Orange Ne-Hi. I quickly thrust the top of the bottle into the silver colored opener below the coin box. As I put the round opening of the bottle onto my parched lips, I could see a boy about 5 years old staring at me. After my initial gulp, I tilted the bottle in his direction and said confidently, "Would you like a swig?" There was a collective gasp in the room. The white man behind the counter shouted, "Don't you do that boy!" I looked at my dad as if to say, "Why not?"

Suddenly I saw a look on my dad's face that I had seen before and it was a look that clearly telegraphed something bad was about to happen. He grabbed the man behind the counter and slammed his face into the cash register and in a single move opened the cash register drawer. He took out three quarters and with an underhand pitch threw them to me. I caught two and one fell to the floor. He lifted the bloody face of the clerk off the register and said, "He is my boy and he is going to buy that boy and the other boy by the door a soda." He then asked, "Do you have a problem with that?" "No sir," said the clerk. Suddenly the sharecroppers moved out of the store and we followed them, me clutching desperately to my orange soda in one hand and my father with my other hand. The sharecroppers formed two lines and we walked between them.

"Dad," I asked, "what happened?" He looked and me and said, "You have the freedom to give that boy a drink and he should have the freedom to take it. That's what happened." It took some time for me to understand that lesson from a veteran of the "The Greatest Generation." I still think of it as I stare inequality down in remote places of the globe.

We walked back in silence to the car and we said nothing to mom and my brother Ron. Dad mounted the spare and drove with one less lug bolt. Mom asked what it cost, he said with that James Copple wry grin, "75 cents." That was my introduction to the price of justice or justice with a fist.

Though my father was hardly a champion of racial tolerance, he was a champion of fairness and choice. My take-away from that experience - in all our efforts to connect with people - regardless of their socio-economic status, the color of their skin or the place of birth, our connections are about covenants and not contracts. I did not offer that boy a drink in anticipation of something in return. I offered because my heart could see in the hot sun of a sweltering Mississippi day that this five-year-old was thirsty and I had a drink that could be shared. I was not afraid of his color, I was not intimidated by my surroundings, rather I was in a moment and the moment demanded a response. There was a bridge between me and that five-year-old child – an empathy path between us.

I spent my early childhood on small farms south and east of Kansas City, Missouri. We were scratch farmers. Farming anywhere between 40 and 150 acres of land. We had a few pigs, chickens, some cattle, a couple of horses and enough land for subsistence farming. It was not a fulltime occupation for my father. He was a milkman on the side. I went to public school and I never thought about the demographics of my classroom - the color of people's skins or their socio-economic status. However, there was one child in my class that everybody knew. He was the banker's kid. Patrick lived in a large ranch-style farmhouse built on a hill. His house overlooked the rest of us. It was about a mile from our farm and part of our property bordered their 640-acre section.

Patrick and I had become friends - I stopped a school bully from picking on him one day and suddenly, I was worthy of his friendship. Then the day came when I received an invitation to a birthday party at his house. My folks did not have enough money to buy a gift, so my mother in an effort to dignify my participation at the party, wrapped an old board game we had inherited in bright colorful paper. Patrick's mother greeted me as I arrived at the party. She was beautiful and I remember that she looked so perfect. I placed my gift on the table with the other gifts. She asked me to remove my shoes because of mud and other "stuff" embedded in the soles of my shoes. The other kids kept their shoes on. I did not recognize many of the children at the party. Later, I discovered many of them attended private schools.

The magical moment came for Patrick to open gifts. I prayed that my gift would be the last - thinking by that time others would be distracted. Rather, he chose my gift first. He opened the gift with anticipation. He looked at it and broke out laughing embarrassing me in the process. I was mortified but stayed the course and declared in front of all these kids that, "I wanted you to have it because it is my favorite game." His mother grabbed the gift and pitched it to the side. I stood there and then watched as he opened his other gifts - all bright, shiny things that everyone loved.

I walked home that day and tried to erase the embarrassment of that experience and thought to myself - how stupid was I to think he would like the gift. Worse, I blamed my mother for setting me up. Didn't she know I would be embarrassed? I walked in the house and she asked, "How was it?" My mother was standing there in a tattered housedress covered in flour. I realized that she had hoped this would be a positive experience for me. I was angry and I wanted to shout at her. I couldn't do it. I said, "Great, he loved the game." I ran to the side of the barn and shouted at the sky.

There was no empathy for me that day. Patrick, his friends, his mother didn't build a bridge to my experience or life. Rather, I felt the weight and the power of their disapproval. I felt small, inadequate and for the first time embarrassment for who and what I was. When I saw my mother - something in my young heart could not blame her. We were different but we were a family that cared for each other and never apologized for who and what we were. That experience has forever served as a reminder that we are to carry the gift of hospitality and compassion. Something in my young heart said, I will do my best never to do that to another person. Out of that experience, God forged, in my heart and mind, a desire and a will to empathize for those who do not, by this world's standards, measure up.

The Structure of our Response

The "professional" humanitarian folk, modify or adjust their (our) language to keep people engaged or because research suggests a different approach. We have gone from serving our neighbor out of a sense of compassion, to aid, to development, to sustainable assistance, and now resiliency. This evolution in thought and approach is important and merits reflection in the context of the voice we hear crying out for help or the voice that simply needs to be heard. Compassion is where it began and, has no doubt been the motivator for helping our neighbor for centuries. It is found in the woman in Kiatine, Kenya that shared her food ration with her neighbor because that is what her neighbor did for her and her family when they were starving. When asked why she did that her response was quick and to the point - "What would Jesus do?"

Eventually, we would institutionalize those responses by creating mechanisms that would provide direct assistance or aid, to those in need. Whether it is our neighbor in suburban Boston or masses of people living in extreme poverty in some forgotten country in the Southern Hemisphere, we contribute something in order to give them something to survive. We have long since learned that aid is a dead-end strategy that only consumes resources but never achieves the objective of lifting someone out of the poverty trap. The poverty trap is any self-reinforcing mechanism that causes poverty to persist. It becomes more and more entrenched when it moves from generation to generation. The trap of poverty expresses itself in systemic ways but also is manifested in personal choices and struggles. It is painful to watch as individuals get caught in the web of self-destruction that only complicates their predicament. *Daily Nation*, a major Kenyan newspaper, published a story of a man hospitalized with severe burns. His wife poured boiling water over him while he was sleeping. She was frustrated by his incessant drinking which left no resources for food. She broke his ribs and gave him a concussion in a previous altercation over his drinking and indifference to the food needs of his family. Now there were medical expenses, legal expenses, and she is being removed from the home. She was an abused woman who struck back - perhaps not appropriately, but in self-defense. The trap continues in this family's journey. The interventions require more than direct aid.

As we hear the voices in our community, our interventions must be guided by compassion but also with the wisdom of producing an intervention that is in fact sustainable. Sustainability is measured by the capacity of the beneficiary and the ownership they assume in response to the aid provided. The more a person participates in the design and implementation of their "rescue" the more likely they will sustain the intervention. Programs and policies are now encouraging us to be sure our work is sustainable. You will not be there for the next challenge or problem - therefore, building the capacity of the individual to guide and direct their own development is critical to long-term health and independence. Whitney Fry, the East Africa Field Director for Strategic Applications International is hyper-sensitive to creating any dependency in our interventions. She looks at each strategy and asks the important question - how sustainable is the intervention and can the individual or the community own it? Recently when developing a Memorandum of Understanding with one of our communities working in Gender-Based Violence, she examined our approach to provide an agricultural or sustainable farming intervention that would provide food and income for women. I had suggested that we pay for the security around the field to protect the crops from thieves or animals. "That is not sustainable," she admonished. "What happens when we run out of money - what will they do? Security is something the community needs to address and resolve so they can maintain it." Spot on! It is important that we maintain that balance between dependence and autonomy in breaking the cycle of poverty or addiction.

The current promising strategy ahead is the role of resiliency. I never met a child or a community that I would completely abandon. I have met angry kids in gangs shouting at the wind because they had no hope. Yet, you begin to peel back the layers of their hopelessness and you find an individual with gifts, a heart for compassion, and an uncanny view of retributive justice. There is a platform for reform, rehabilitation, and reconstruction. The human spirit is an amazing design. Extreme poverty is complicated and often made more complicated by our failure to listen or to understand how creative and imaginative the poor must be to survive. I have never seen such creativity! Again, it is in children that we see it so wonderfully manifested. In the most extreme conditions of poverty and violence, I have seen children running through the streets laughing and playing with hand-made toys or old tires. Kids find old tires and run through the streets rolling them as if to see how far they can go before the tire falls to the ground. The laughter and the giggling are always present. Engraved in my memory is a child in the Baba Dogo slum of Nairobi standing next to a sewer stream of gray water filled with medical and electronic waste from a nearby factory. As I walked by his corrugated tin roof homestead, a smile broke out that was an image of pure innocence and wonder. I love and I am amazed at the contradiction found in the laughter of a child or children in the chaos and frenetic pace of survival in communities of poverty.

Resiliency is something that can be measured and is present in the most horrific conditions. Recently Amanda, Michelle, and Gina were held for ten years in a single homestead in Cleveland, Ohio. Captives of a perverted sex addict who tortured and bound them in chains. Yet, when the time was right, their inner strength, their character, and resiliency led them to their escape. What would appear to most of us to be a hopeless or impossible situation - the individual spirit rallied as one escaped through an unlocked door to cry for help. A neighbor heard and responded to their cry and effected the rescue. It will take time - but they will be restored and they will recover. The scar tissue from the experience will forever be present but hopefully, it will not dictate their future. Their experience seems so remote and abstract that it is difficult to grasp the horror of their situation. How could people for ten years be held captive? The empathy bridge is hard to construct until we start peeling back the facts and getting beyond our first impressions. What did they experience, how did they feel, and what gave them hope? These questions help construct the bridge between us and the individuals we seek to rescue.

Regardless of the strategies we employ, the most effective and enduring rescue is one that is driven by an empathic impulse. Again, it can be dangerous and demand responses that take us out of our comfort zone. Regardless, it is the expression of a living faith that fuels compassion and action. Empathy requires us to come alongside an individual or community and to walk with them in their journey. It requires us to live "incarnationally," en-fleshed in a world that is broken and in need of healing. Empathy is possible in our lives when we are prepared to abandon the normal indicators of success or failure. Our work is about the inutility of service not the measures of success often required by donors and weak-minded politicians.

As a young 19 year-old sent to Bolivia for a summer mission experience, I came across the first tangible foreign experience that would define my journey into empathic responses to children and poverty. Traveling with missionary nurse, Linda Spaulding, I arrived in a village where a young girl had an eye infection caused by rubbing her eyes with soiled hands, often covered in feces. Linda, very casually informed me that the child would not survive. We went about our work. I took her picture and three days later, we traveled back through that village to find a mother in mourning over the death of her child. I felt a piece of me died that day - and yet I also found a fire ignited in my soul that would forever define my decisions for the future. I sought to feel with that mother and to put myself in her place. There would always be a separation as I am not that mother. However, taking my own experience of loss and grief (though limited) into that context allowed me to think more clearly about solutions to the poverty that caused her child's death. Any other approach is simply formulaic and sterile.

As we take this journey, my faith gives me both strength and comfort to know that I do not go alone. It is the empathic bridge between God and man that allows me to feel and to act empathically without being destroyed by the emotions of the experience or environment.

"Though I walk through the valley of the shadow of death - you are with me." That *you are with me* promise jumps off the page and seizes my heart and my head every time I read it. I have certainly witnessed that promise on more than one occasion. In extreme cases, whether traversing a dangerous road in Bolivia, Haiti, or Ethiopia or listening at my daughter's bedside to the doctors describe her preeclampsia and just how close she was to death - **you are with me**. In good seasons - in bad seasons -

in all seasons - *you are with me*. Does it get any better than that?

For the past several weeks, I have witnessed the lives of men and women working in the valleys of death. The shadows have been long and often leading others to despair. They move through these valleys with a confidence and hope that brings relief to those in hunger, loneliness or fear for their lives. They walk among the displaced in Internally Displaced People (IDP) camps; they comfort the refugee; they listen to the fear expressed because there is no money for food or water; they watch as people fear a future where an election could produce violence; they wonder who will be living or who will be dead the next time they enter this valley.

You are with me becomes the road beneath their feet. *You are with me* makes it possible for them to go, *you are with me* is what brings a healing embrace, *you are with me* is what allows them to transcend the pain and the hurt of the world they have chosen to serve. *You are with me* allows me to feel a grace and forgiveness that cuts through my humanity and my fallible and broken choices.

Today, I go through several valleys where the shadow of death conceals the beauty of life. Yet, though I walk through those valleys, I go with a hope and a confidence that *you are with me*. With that - I can do this - with that promise, despair becomes hope. With that promise, the clouds that produce the shadows evaporate and the horizon becomes something to anticipate not fear. ***You are with me***. Think about it - what does that promise mean to you?

The Judgment Wall

In this work, we humans find it easier to judge than to feel empathy or to practice forgiveness. I find it easy to judge and to build walls that segregate the good guys from the bad. I find it easy to blame the alcoholic for his abusive behavior or the pastoralist woman starving on the plains of Turkana when she chooses to abandon younger children so the older children can help forage for food. My judgment can be harsh. I am committed to practicing justice, loving mercy and when possible, walking humbly with my God. Humility is not one of my great attributes. When seeking justice, there are conclusions that define good behavior from bad behavior.

Where there is no forgiveness, there is no empathy; where there is no empathy - we sow the fertile ground of injustice and reap isolation. Forgiveness must begin with ourselves recognizing that we must first become a forgiven and redeemed soul. It is not by our work, but by His grace that we engage or triumph. By no means, does this lead us into perfect responses. I am crushed by "holy" people that claim certain aspects of perfection, but fail to see that we must engage in justice enterprises that change culture, governments, and corporate norms.

The current political environment which pushes constituents to rush to judgment but fails to understand the journey of the opposition has become toxic and contaminates our discourse. In the 2008 political campaign, I saw postings on Facebook making fun of Senator and presidential candidate John McCain and ridiculing him because he could not bend his arms. What they did not realize was that McCain was tortured and beaten mercilessly for years in a prison during the Vietnam War. He did this serving his country and for us to ridicule his injuries - no empathic bridge can be constructed. Empathy takes us off our perch and puts us alongside the broken and the oppressed. The voice from the night somehow harmonizes with our voice to rescue. Beyond simple rescue, the voice from the night becomes our invitation to walk alongside a child, a family, or community.

As I write these final words, I am in Nairobi, Kenya closely monitoring news reports about an F5 Tornado that has ripped through the community of Moore, Oklahoma. As of this moment, 24 people are dead and the tornado, two miles in width, left a path of destruction that destroyed homes, businesses, schools, and churches. On Facebook this morning, the normal banter about graduations, birthdays, weddings, and frivolous commentary about politics gives way to calls for help. The calls for help are met by "friends" urging donations and offering prayers of support. Throughout the next days, the empathy bridge will be built and as we hear stories of those killed, those who lost homes, and those whose lives are forever altered by ten minutes of life-threatening wind, we will travel across that bridge and turn our feelings into action. Our pocketbooks will open, our donations will increase, and our hands will offer assistance driven by hearts that are broken.

When you hear the voices from the night, they may seem distant because they are not our kin or our neighbor, but they are our brothers and sisters in humanity. We may turn away from the appeals of organizations working alongside those voices because they are repetitive or too harsh to observe, but if we allow ourselves to hear with our hearts, to see with our hearts, and to act with our hearts, the voices become our voices and our voices become theirs. That experience is empathy - but it is also transformative!

Statistics for this chapter were taken from the *Sunday New York Times Magazine*, August 23, 2009 pp 28-43.

See Jeremy Sachs, *The End of Poverty*, Penguin Books for an extensive analysis of the Poverty Trap.

Chapter Nine - Making It Happen

Most of us working in the areas of poverty eradication or in child or vulnerable population advocacy do not have a problem with motivation. Translating motivation into action that is sustainable is what ultimately changes the world. Think globally but act locally is a mantra often repeated by advocates. For good reason - it really is the only way you can make a difference. If you are inspired to get involved then we suggest some immediate and measurable activities that would take you from talk to action.

Things *You* Can Do

1. You can listen to the children in your neighborhoods. Listen to them in the various venues you meet or encounter them - the school, the church, the playing field, after-school activities, or in your home.

2. Identify yourself as an advocate for children and vulnerable populations so people know your passion.

3. Ask concrete and specific questions about the systems that are designed to protect the welfare of our most at risk children. These would include feeding

programs, literacy initiatives, and access to after-school activities.

4. Watch media reports and follow-up with the organizations working in the lives of children.

5. Meet with children in their neighborhood and school settings. Attend community events where children are engaged or involved. Demonstrate to your neighbors and friends that you are serious about volunteerism and becoming involved.

6. Meet with parents of children exposed to violence, crime, and substance abuse and work with them, not against them, in developing strategies for intervention or treatment.

7. Contribute to youth serving organizations.

8. Engage lawmakers and policy makers around these critical issues.

Things Your *Community* or *Organization* can do

1. Do everything that an individual could and should do.

2. Incorporate the strategic planning process of your collaboration or

coalition language that emphasizes deliverance and rescue.

3. Engage organizations that could assist in the development of a cost analysis of juvenile crime, violence, and treatment. Get at the reality of what it is costing your community.

4. Devise media strategies that promote the condition and welfare of your community's children.

5. Involve children and youth in your community and organizational planning processes.

6. Be sure you major corporations or businesses in your community have corporate social responsibility programs.

7. Build on inclusivity. Promote activities that involve the greatest number of children.

8. Be sensitive to diversity, gender, and socio-economic status when you are designing programs or projects.

9. Meet regularly with policy makers (City Council, County Commission, State Legislators, and Federal Policy Makers) to discuss critical issues and how they can help. Be specific.

Things We Can Do as a *Nation* or *People*

1. Hold all elected officials accountable for their rhetoric about children.
2. Monitor local, state, and national budget priorities for children.
3. Promote a Global Child Protection Act that binds all UN member nations to prioritize child education and welfare. Revisit the Millennium Development Goals and monitor your nation's commitment to their completion.
4. Be sure your country is a signature on all UN Charters for Human Rights and Child and Women Protection.
5. Identify multi-national corporations and appeal to the Corporate Social Responsibility Offices to engage in child protection and advocacy.
6. Promote youth participation in all governing bodies to better ascertain and to represent the interests of young peo ple.

Acknowledgments

I recently finished a book on wealth and property in the early Medieval Church. The acknowledgement section was fifteen pages long. I am tempted - but I will restrain myself. There are so many individuals, including the individuals and characters described in *Voices from the Night* whose lives, character, and strength inspired this writing, but more importantly, shaped my life. My partners, clients, and collaborators gave me the opportunities and the context for this book. They are often mentioned throughout the book. I would be remiss if I failed to mention the intellectual mentors that shaped my career and help direct my life to one of service. Those include but not limited to, James R. Cameron, Paul Bassett, the late Timothy L. Smith, Jocelyn Hillgarth, Ronald J. Sider, Vera Hance, and Ray Lunn Hance.

I want to thank Amy Crofford. Amy is by far and away the finest editor I have ever engaged. She is an instructional editor and her process makes you a better writer. Amy is a missionary in the Church of the Nazarene who I met while working in Kenya. She is smart, analytical, and a writer's conscience on so many levels. Amy and her husband, Greg, spent hours editing, discussing, and sometimes arguing with me on the substance and merits of my writing.

Sara Mesa designed the cover and oversaw the details of the publication and website that supports this book. She has been my collaborator and assistant on so many different projects. Her friendship and contribution to our work has made us look good in the face of many potential disasters.

Finally, I want to acknowledge my wife and life partner, Colleen Kay Copple. She heard many of the same voices I heard on this journey. She is my filter, my counselor, and my guide in all of life.

Ultimately, in the world of electronic publishing, when you hit the "send" button, it is the writer and the writer alone that bears the responsibility for what is before you. Nobody feels that responsibility more than this writer. Forgive my errors, celebrate the good news and feel free to email me at jcopple@sai-dc.com if you want to discuss or challenge any conclusions in this book.